Family

E V E R   A F T E R

Family
EVER AFTER

SIMPLE WAYS TO ACHIEVE
EXTRAORDINARY HAPPINESS WITH
YOUR ORDINARY FAMILY

MICHELLE H. PACKARD

Copyright © 2012 by Michelle H. Packard
All rights reserved.
Published by Familius LLC, www.familius.com
Familius books are available at special discounts for bulk purchases for sales promotions, family, or corporate use. Special editions, including personalized covers, excerpts of existing books, or books with corporate logos, can be created in large quantities for special needs. For more information, contact Premium Sales at 801-552-7298 or email specialmarkets@familius.com

Library of Congress Catalog-in-Publication Data
2013933808

pISBN 9781938301384
eISBN 9781938301391

Physical book printed in the United States of America
Book design by Dana Knudsen and Maggie Wickes
Cover design by David Miles
Edited by Dana Knudsen and Maggie Wickes
Vector Images by Clarice Gomes Designs

First Edition

This book is dedicated to all my family. May your *Ever Afters* be extraordinary. It is also dedicated to every Disney Princess who had a dysfunctional family and still lived happily *ever after*.

Table of Contents

Acknowledgments 1

Preface. 3

Ever After 7

Happiness through Perspective. 13

Deceived 21

Defining What's Important .31

Tick-Tock. 49

Our Family through Our Eyes. 67

Peace is Persuasive: Resolving Conflict 85

Great Expectations. 117

We Grow Funny Looking Cucumbers 139

Extending the Love 155

Love Fosters Love 167

Bibliography. 181

About the Author. 183

About Familius. 185

Acknowledgments

As I anxiously hit the send button, I took a quick inventory of myself. My hair was oily and frazzled, I hadn't put makeup on for days, I was wearing my baggy blue sweat pants and had emptied two bottles of Nutella by the spoonful. I was locked away in the corner of my bedroom, ignoring everything around me, and was a total disaster.

When I started writing *Family Ever After,* I spent hours pouring over books about writing. I was assured that I didn't need to be the crazy with tousled hair, living off of cappuccinos, alone in some remote corner in order to be a writer. It was a lie. I didn't even know it was happening until the transformation was complete.

To all you authors out there, kudos. I never imagined it would be so difficult. I truly couldn't have done it without my mom, who made a special trip to watch the kids so I could evolve into a crazy and unkempt person alone in my bedroom, and to both my parents for living happily ever after, even when it was hard. A special thanks to James and Jodi Hutchings for their hours of editing and critical thinking and to Marquie and Patrick Walton for sticking with me until the end. A big thank you to Maggie Wickes and Dana Knudsen for their editing and patience with my lack of skills. So much thanks goes to Patrick and Rick Walton for finding me, to David Miles for his brilliant vision on the cover, and to Christopher Robbins and the rest of the Familius family. The work you do really does make families happier. Thank you to many friends and family who have shared personal stories and have taught me what happily ever after really means. Lots of love and thank yous to my kids for their patience and help. Extra gratitude to my husband for giving me his time when he had none to give— you'll always be my favorite!

Preface

As I go from place to place living out my daily activities, I love to observe people. I watch them at the mall, grocery store, school, business place, and home. There is so much to see and so much to learn. I have noticed of late that people often appear tired and unhappy. I have spoken with hundreds of people on the topic of life and happiness and have received many depressing and discouraging responses, and I can't help but wonder why. I, too, have days where I experience little enthusiasm for my daily routine, and have realized on these particular days, I find myself feeling lonely, tired, and rushed. This has led me to ask: what has happened to our peace and our happiness? My observations, both of myself and of others, have instilled in me a desire to help bring peace and happiness back to the heart and home.

Obviously, this book is not intended to solve the world's problems or cure sickness and mental disorders, but I trust that it will give hope for a happier life. I believe that hope in a happier life comes from having happier homes and families. I wonder what the world would look like if we went to the store and were thinking of someone we love. I wonder how schools would change if students knew their parents supported them, were invested in their lives, and loved them more than anything. I wonder how the business place would feel if everyone showed as much commitment to their spouses as they did to their bosses. I wonder how the home would be if people spent their time and energy showing love to those they love the most. What if people could find peace and happiness despite the imperfection in their lives and families? Our families affect all aspects of our lives, and if we have happy families, I feel it is safe to say we will have happy lives.

I can think of no better way to display this principle than through the example of my own parents. As my father was mowing the lawn one day, he unexpectedly found himself in a wrestling match with the lawn mower. Miraculously, despite the tumble of man and mower, he walked away with only a broken arm, sore muscles, scrapes, and a few bruises. About five days after the accident, I called to see how he was doing. He informed me that he was at the dentist with my mother, who had just had a root canal. He told me that he was worried about her because she had injured her knees, and was hoping for her to take care of the injury quickly before it caused her further pain. He spoke not of his own injuries, but of his wife's current battle; it was so heartfelt and so sweet. I couldn't help but think, "I love that my mom and dad are so invested and concerned for one another when both are dealing with great challenges. I love that, though it is difficult at times, they take care of each other. I love that they still love each other." Even though they are in pain and still busy with work, grandchildren, and other responsibilities, they have discovered the key to peace and happiness. They are living happily *ever after*.

There is nothing extraordinary about my parents. They started the journey of their *ever after* the same way as the rest of us did. They have not been immune to tragedy, stress, loneliness, or failures, and yet they have found extraordinary happiness in life by showing love to the ones they love the most.

As I have written this book, I have noticed a marked change in the happiness of my marriage, my home, my family, and my life as I am reminded daily of a better, happier way. It doesn't matter what type of family you are from; the principles in this book will help you if you come from a traditional family, or if you are single, widowed, or divorced, and it will help you whether you have children or not. Your *ever after* will be what you make of it. Let this book be a guide to you as you invest yourself in your *ever after* and make it a happy one.

As you read, you will come across many personal experiences that others have shared. Many of their names have been changed as well as male/female tenses, in order to protect their privacy.

CHAPTER ONE

Ever After

Challenge: Write down how you picture your happily ever after

As I lay in bed with sleepy eyes and little motivation to rise from my slumber, I couldn't help but notice my husband still asleep next to me and think, "Why don't I want to make him a special dinner, go on a date with him, or be romantic?" As I pondered these questions, I wondered, "What happened to our happily *ever after*?" It seemed like just yesterday that I was gazing at my 'soon to be' with total devotion—almost to the point of worshiping him. In my eyes, he had been perfect and so handsome. I had twirled in my flowing white dress and felt like a princess. I had smiled that everlasting smile, the smile that lasts through the wedding, the luncheon, and the reception. It was the kind of smile that made your cheeks hurt just as much as your feet. I had breathed in the beauty of that lovely day, and had let a tear roll down my cheek. I had thought I was the luckiest girl in the world. I had never imagined someone could love me so deeply, and I had never imagined those feelings would ever fade.

As we honeymooned, we explored our new expressions of freedom. We could be, do, and become whatever we wanted and manifest our love in whatever way we liked. I pictured us growing old together, hand in hand as we walked life's scenic paths. I saw my white picket fence, my perfectly behaved children happily playing behind it. I saw a successful and delightful family. Our honeymoon should have lasted forever, but work got busy, friends resurfaced, bills had to be paid, and we wanted to have children. We began to ease ourselves back into reality and out of our newlywed bubble. It was not bad, just not as perfect as I had imagined.

As the pace of life quickened, our waistlines began to expand, our hairlines began to recede, and the stress of life began to creep in. As our children joined our lives, our bed became the communal sleep fortress for our children and we forgot what it was like to have a solid night of rest. We would blow a kiss and holler an 'I love you' as we passed through the portal of our home. There seemed to be a constant time lapse between us and we could never land ourselves in the same place at the same time. My happily *ever after* was quickly transforming into a heap of work, and I found myself thinking, "This is not what I signed up for—this is not how I pictured happily *ever after*." Then I realized, maybe this *is* what I signed up for and I just don't know how to make my *ever after* happy. I began to wonder, if perhaps it *is* possible to have a happily *ever after*, even when my white picket fence is broken, my 'beautiful' lawn is dead, and my children are less than angelic.

This unexpected realization of hope was not without precedent in my life. Similarly, as I had prepared to go to college, I had been smothered with warnings: "It is so hard," "don't give up," or "you can do it." I, of course, was all confidence and not the least bit worried. As my first finals approached, in my sleep-deprived state, the stress of school tumbled down onto me and I quickly realized my previous visions of an easy and blissful college experience were flawed. I had then thought to myself, "This is really hard." The same is true in marriage and family life. Nothing can prepare us for such a lengthy road of dedication; the only way to experience and understand family life is to live it.

When I spoke to my baby sister two months after her marriage, she told me about an exceptionally discouraging argument she had with her husband. In desperation she had burst out, "I don't know how to be married!" This couple had spent months preparing for marriage. They had discussed every family life topic they could conjure up; they had taken marriage preparation classes, and they had seen each other in just about every circumstance imaginable. They had received solicited and not so solicited advice and tried to listen, but still they felt unprepared. The happiest couples I know, many whom have been married ten, twenty, and thirty or more years still have moments when they just don't know what to do, and they find themselves saying, "*this is really hard!*"

Family life is like riding the white rickety roller coaster at the amusement park, the one you are sure is going to tumble down before you finish the ride. Your journey begins when you make a commitment and jump into the roller coaster. It is so exhilarating to strap your belt on, clasp hands with the one you love, and begin the climb. As you get to know each other, you discover he leaves hair shavings in the sink and she leaves makeup powder on the counter.

You climb to the first peak with butterflies in your stomach. You have no idea what to expect, but you hope once you get to the top, the hardest part will be over. It is both horrifying and thrilling at the same time. You roll over the apex and a nonsensical ride looms before you. You realize in that tiny moment it is not going to be the smooth coast to the end that you imagined.

The honeymoon is over, you throw your hands in the air, your stomach is in your throat, and you are flying faster than you thought humanly possible. You slam into a turn—you have a new baby, no insurance, and school loans—it hurts. Suddenly, there is a brief moment of peace—as you enjoy a romantic weekend with your hubby, your son makes the football team, you get a great new job, or you finally potty train your three-year-old. Without warning, you are spinning in a circle—running kids here and there, volunteering to coach the Pee Wee football team, scrambling for enough money to pay the bills, and cleaning up your neighbor's shattered window that your son shot a rock through.

For a moment, your cart feels claustrophobic and you envision yourself suffocating under the pressure of life as you have a major blow out with your husband over disciplining the kids. As your stomach begins to churn, you realize you are at the top of a giant loop-de-loop. You have lost your thirst for adventure and are wondering, "Am I really going to make it?" More than anything, you want the ride to end. You want to feel human again, you want peace, and you need love. You begin to wonder, "Is there any way to get off this ride?" Instinctively, you know the only way is to jump, and you know that would be catastrophic, so somehow you stay strapped in, and you keep going.

Through all the ups and downs, twists and bends, the kids grow up and move out and you unexpectedly find yourself back at the beginning. You are left where you started with only the two of you in your slowing cart, and you think to yourself, "*What a ride!*" You begin to look at the family photos and reminisce with fondness about how loud you screamed and how your stomachs dropped when you flew through the last loop-de-loop. As you survey the panorama of your life while squeezing the hand of the one you love so deeply, you find in the end you are an entirely altered person, a better person. You are better because you held tighter when things were hard, you sacrificed, and you let love overpower all obstacles. You are delighted you jumped in the cart so many years before and realize your happiness wasn't found in your destination but rather in the crazy ride.

Happily *ever afters* don't just happen; they must be made. There will be unforeseen bends and bumps. No marriage or family is free from exhaustion, financial struggle, argument, disappointment, tragedy, or heartache. We all have mornings when we wake up and wonder, "Who is this person I married, and what have I gotten myself into?" Maybe things in your family are good but could be better. Maybe you feel like your family is broken or maybe you think they are so annoying you can't stand to be with them. Maybe you're depressed, or you always feel exhausted. There are numerous difficulties and detours on the road to *ever after*. Whatever your personal situation, the good news is there are things we can all do to make the burden lighter, and to have a stronger, happier family.

Equip yourself with extra pillows when you climb onto the rickety roller coaster. Bring forgiveness, compassion, patience, humor, and extra love. You will need all the cushion you can get. Hold tight to forgiveness when your husband says something stupid, or your wife doesn't show gratitude for your hard work. Pack some compassion for the moments your children are embarrassed at school or your daughter doesn't make the team. Bring patience for that hundredth time you have to convince your kids to brush their teeth and put on their pajamas. Find humor in the mundane, and when you are uncertain about what to do, stuff in all the extra love you have to offer. Let these pillows soften the blows of family life's sharp turns. Find comfort in them; let them heal you when you think you can't make it, and relish them when things are good.

Everyone's picture of happily *ever after* is different. My happily *ever after* is doing dishes with my husband and simply being happy to do it, sliding down a mountain on my bum and ripping a hole in my pants while my husband laughs at me because I'm too scared to walk down. It is watching my kids splash in the pool, their deep, carefree laughs filling the air. It is waking up Christmas morning to a house full of balloons, or lying on my husband's shoulder feeling safe and protected. It is the joy that engulfs me when my family knows I love them, and the peace that comes from knowing how much they love me. This is not the *ever after* I imagined years ago, as the satin folds of my white sparkling princess dress twirled around me and I was lost in my husband's brown eyes. Nor is it what I imagined during our short honeymoon bliss. This is better because this is real. Find your vision of *ever after* and live it; you may be surprised to find the journey is the part you love the most.

CHAPTER TWO

Happiness through Perspective

*Challenge: Find an opportunity to carry out the
Red Punch Experiment*

The Red Punch Experiment

Our perfectly envisioned happily *ever after* does not come from fairy tales. It is not in a dream or a wish. *The perfection and happiness we long for in family life is found in our perspective.* How we treat our family is a manifestation of how we perceive them. When we are first married, we love our spouse perfectly. Though imperfections are rampant, we are able to look past little faults, like the pile of dirty laundry on the floor or the backseat driving. We spend our time looking for thoughtful things to do for each other rather than looking for ways to fix each other. Ten years down the road, when our husband still throws his clothes on the floor, it is no longer endearing. Our spouse hasn't changed, but our perspective has. We clearly see every fault of our loved one and are no longer patient with the pile of laundry or the paranoid woman in the passenger seat.

Allow me to introduce the Red Punch Experiment, a tool to find happiness for you and for your family despite imperfections. I fell upon this idea in one of my college classes and have catered it to my own life. Let me set the scene: As company arrives, I finish preparing my favorite gourmet meal and admire my beautifully set table. I vacuum the floor, fluff the couch pillows, and hide the remaining dirty dishes in the dishwasher. As I dash away to put on a clean shirt, I remember to brush my teeth, touch up my makeup, and ensure the kids have spotless rooms (that no one will ever see). The guests are at the door; I graciously invite them in and we begin a delicious and lovely meal.

As we enjoy dinner, our guest bumps over his glass of red wine. It pours across the table, soaks his pants and speckles the floor and chair with a vibrant red. I jump up and say, "Let me get a towel." Flustered and damp, our guest apologizes profusely. As I clean the carpet, I assure him all is well. The mess and embarrassment are wiped away with love and some absorbent towels. Dinner resumes and eventually finishes with cheerfulness; no real harm has been done, save the issue of those soggy pants. When the evening is over, I am tired but I am definitely satisfied with the successful night, even if there is a red stain on the chair.

Now, let's observe a similar scene. I get home from work, the kids are hungry, and I am tired. After throwing on my lounge pants and t-shirt, I whip out some of my very best cans of soup, divvy out my least stale crackers, and mix a quick pitcher of Kool-Aid for a swift and easy dinner. The kids are moaning about their empty stomachs, and I am wholly distracted by what a wreck the house is in when, in a careless moment, one of the kids bumps their glass of Kool-Aid. Just as the wine decorated the tablecloth, chair, clothing, and floor, so does the Kool-Aid. Words fly out of my mouth at an unstoppable pace: "What were you thinking? Why did you leave your glass on the edge? We are never going to get this stain out!" As I impatiently command my child to get a towel, the tension rises and my perception of happiness is obstructed. All I can see is an abundance of red, flooding over an already daunting mountain of chores.

Oh, the moments like these! How I wish I could take them back. In that instant, though my family wasn't inherently unhappy, I did not perceive or find happiness in them. I expected perfection and I had no patience for human error. My kids annoyed me and cleaning up that glass of Kool-Aid was just one more tally mark on my "I'm never going to make it to my happily *ever after*" list. On the other hand, I perceived our friends to be worthy of a wonderful meal, a clean house, and a compassionate disposition toward the spilled wine. It wasn't a big deal that they spilled the wine because I cared more about them than I did about the stain on the chair.

Family life presents us with the opportunity to turn diamonds in the rough to priceless gems. But if we ignore our family or are too hard on them, our gems may lose their luster. How then do we show them they are vital to us, that they are number one—more important than anything or anyone? The refining and polishing of our imperfect diamonds is done as we perceive our loved ones clearly and treat them as priceless and valuable. When situations arise in your family, think to yourself, "Am I treating my family better than my friends? When I act this way do they know I love them?" Then, adjust your actions accordingly. Show love to the ones you love the most by perceiving them and treating them as worthy to receive such love.

I remember when my sweet kiddo fell and scraped her knee. She had been playing with the neighbor, and when she came in crying, I verified she was okay and told her she would be fine. My quick scan satisfied me that there was no permanent damage, so I sent her on her way and resumed my previous activity. Later on that same day, the neighbor girl poked a stick under her fingernail. I quickly sympathized because I knew how badly that hurts and used my finest first aid skills wrapping that sore nail with double Band-Aids just to make sure it would stay covered and clean. Although I was more than satisfied with my handiwork, my heart sank as I realized I had taken better physical and emotional care of the neighbor than of my own daughter. In this instance, I failed the Red Punch Experiment.

Recently, I caught my son playing on the Wii after I had expressly forbidden him to do so. I turned it off and he exploded with anger. I was mellow and spoke kindly. I explained why I had turned off the Wii and administered what I considered fair and appropriate discipline. During his discipline, I called him sweetheart, and he was baffled. In a put-out voice, he asked, "Why did you call me sweetheart when I am in trouble?" I told him, "Even though you did something wrong I still love you, and still enjoy you. You have to learn that actions have consequences, but even when you make mistakes I will always love you." Red Punch Experiment success!

The All-Encompassing Effects of the Red Punch Experiment

This experiment is all-encompassing. It isn't just for the kids; it's for the spouse, siblings, and in-laws as well. It is for the single parents and for the couple without children. It can be used by anyone, for anyone in your family.

One night, my husband was trying to have a relaxing evening with me. He just wanted to watch a movie. I was up for it, but the pile of laundry in my family room was calling for my attention, and I knew I wouldn't be able to focus on a movie. So I thought to myself, "I can hit two birds with one stone," and I began to fold while the movie played. My husband had been digging dirt and lifting heavy equipment all day. He was exhausted and just desired my attention. As I innocently folded laundry, he was feeling guilty for not helping. I sincerely didn't care if he helped or not, but I just didn't want to wake up to a pile of unfolded laundry. As we continued, my husband was growing frustrated with me, and all I could think was, "What's the big deal?"

Luckily, I decided that I wanted him to know he was more important to me than that pile of laundry, because hello . . . he is. While I felt that what I was doing was harmless, his perception of the situation was different and he felt like I wasn't giving him the love he needed. I realized our perceptions could easily be compared to an optical illusion. What we saw depended on the angle from which we viewed the situation, our proximity to it, and the amount of time we spent analyzing it. This means we will likely perceive the same situation and outcome differently than our spouses or children on more than a few occasions. Remember, it is all in our perception. I soon realized my husband and I were not seeing or finding happiness in the same things, but we could still be happy and love each other at the same time.

Since I desired happiness for both of us, without anger or resentment I simply said, "I love you more than this pile of laundry and I will stop folding." Of course, this reaction made him feel guiltier. I assured him again that it was really okay and I would rather love him than do the laundry. With that, he helped me fold the laundry and then we cuddled and watched a movie. My husband later informed me he helped with the laundry because he decided I was more important than the movie, his tired limbs, or his preconceived ideas of how the night should be.

This may sound cheesy but it really worked. My husband felt loved and happy and I felt helped and happy. Laundry is the chore I loathe above all others. I was relieved not to have that pile of clothes awaiting me and was able to enjoy the rest of the evening. However, even if my husband had not decided to help with the laundry, I would have been content to let it wait until morning. When attempting to show love to the ones you love the most, be sincere. I speak from experience because my family can see right through me. They know when I mean what I say, when I am playing the martyr, or when I'm putting them on a guilt trip.

Kindness Fosters Happiness

So why does the Red Punch Experiment—showing love and kindness to the ones we love the most—bring happiness to our *ever after*? Dr. Decia Dixon, licensed psychologist, explains in her blog, "Happy Children and Families," that when people show kindness, it helps them and their loved ones feel peace and gives them hope that their families can be successful, that people are good despite their weaknesses, and that love given and received can facilitate positive outcomes (Dixon, 2012). When we show love and kindness to the ones we love the most, it helps us to feel happy and feel like we can do hard things like have a family. It also helps us look past the hard times and perceive a bright future with our family.

One of the great things about friends is that they don't usually live with us, and we don't have to deal with their oddities and idiosyncrasies day in and day out. If we are tired of them or they keep spilling punch on the carpet, we can go home or send them home, but our families are forever buzzing around us. Because families are so near to us so much of the time, they have a special way of exasperating us faster and more efficiently than anyone else. I remember telling my husband in a heated dispute that he brings out the worst in me. I let him know my siblings couldn't even irritate me like he could. Family doesn't go away. In fact, sometimes I think they stay just to annoy us. The beauty in family life is that we can choose not to be annoyed and instead to love our family and find happiness with them.

Do we perceive our family and treat them as if they are diamonds in the rough, full of spectacular and sensational potential, or do we perceive and treat them as if they are hindering our world? Do we treat them like our honored guests or do we see ourselves as martyrs in our own homes? Our family is our world and deserves our best love. It is essential that we treat and see our families as though they are more significant and more important than the red stain on the chair. Our perceptions will dictate our own satisfaction, and our actions regarding those perceptions will shape the attitudes, behaviors, and reactions of our entire family. If we see our families as perfect in all their imperfections and love and treat them accordingly, we will find our happily *ever after* because we will be happy with what we see and what we have. Our families will find joy and love as they perceive themselves to be our number one priority.

One discouraging evening, my husband was depressed about his imperfect parenting and family until he had a sudden change in perspective. He realized perfect parenting and family life is not found in perfect children, perfect parents, or a perfect home, but that a perfect parent or family is one in which spouse and children know they are loved.

We can't always live at a perfect level. Our house isn't always going to be clean, and sometimes we eat canned soup and stale crackers for dinner. It really isn't about what we eat or how fancy the table is set, but how we perceive and treat our family. Did we bring our pillows full of forgiveness, compassion, patience and love on the ride of our life? Friends are vital and we love them, but our family is there for the long haul. No matter how much they manage to burrow under our skin, they really are and really should be our number one priority. The most valuable gems are unique, and we love them for that uniqueness. They are perfect in their imperfection. We protect them, we care for them, and in turn they bring us happiness.

CHAPTER THREE

Deceived

Challenge: Look for a deception you have created and examine a new perspective

on't lose your perspective in deception. Often, we trap ourselves by our inability to see beyond our own tunnel vision. The Arbinger Institute suggests that we put ourselves "in a box," and we can't get out of that theoretical box, because the perceptions we have already created blind us, making it so that we don't even know there is anything on the other side of our box (Arbinger, 2010). In order to see things as they are and as they should be for our families, we must acknowledge that it is time to broaden our horizons and look outside of our individual boxes. A change in our perspective could be monumentally important in living our happily *ever after* because this change forces us to examine what life is like for our loved ones. An even more important and powerful change may be to examine the role we play in those lives.

This concept of looking outside the box can apply to both large and small things. I think of my own, perhaps silly example of perception and deception. I used to see parents put their kids on leashes when they went out, and I definitely had something negative to say about that! What kind of parent would put their kid on a leash? Children are not animals, I maintained, and should not be put on leashes simply because it's easier for the parent. When my oldest child disappeared at the mall, my perspective about these leashes changed in a single moment and I was forced to look beyond my tunnel vision. When I found out she was missing, I thought, "Oh, she is just right here, probably on the other side of that rack." My search expanded rapidly through the store, until I was in a full-on panic. I notified the store clerk, who initiated a Code Adam (in which everyone stops what they are doing and looks for the lost child), but alas, she was not in the store. I didn't know it at that moment, but she was on her way to see the sparkling Christmas tree at the other end of the mall.

If you have ever lost a child when you have been out and about, you know that sick, plummeting feeling where the fear of the unknown sets in and tightens around your neck and you have to remind yourself to breathe. It brings with it an abrupt onset of paranoia and panic, as well as regret and anger that you didn't watch your child more diligently. To my total relief, an angel of a woman found my daughter that day and I then discovered the beauty, ease, and peace of mind of the "child leash." I discovered it could give children their desired freedom while protecting them, an element that gives peace to their parents.

I was entirely in my 'box' about the child leash. I had deceived myself by my own unwillingness to alter my perspective, creating a potentially ominous situation for my family. We cannot put iron bars of ignorance around ourselves and effectively function. We need to keep our perspectives malleable, expand our horizons, and think to ourselves, "How would I feel if I were in their situation?", "Does it really matter if they do things differently than me?", or "Is there more than one way to view and handle the circumstance?" Our new, broadened perspectives may allow us to learn things that can transform our relationships with the people who are most important to us.

If you are a parent or a spouse, it is likely you are endlessly going, doing, and serving. Sometimes, we fool ourselves into thinking that we give so much we couldn't possibly be selfish. However, if we closely examine ourselves, it is likely we will find room for a few more apologies, a little more love, and a broader perspective. Our levels of selfishness and selflessness are places where we are often highly prone to self-deception, and as family members, we often find ourselves flirting with the line between one and the other. It is important to remember that taking care of yourself isn't selfish. Having alone time without your kids or your spouse isn't selfish. Having needs and hopes and dreams isn't selfish, but thinking that you are the only one with needs, hopes, and dreams is selfish.

Before you read on, write out these four lists:

1. Your hopes, dreams, and goals (both short- and long-term).

2. Your family members and their goals, hopes, and dreams.

3. How your goals from list one affect the people and their goals, hopes, and dreams in list two. How do your family's goals and needs align with yours?

Note: If your goals do not align with that of your family, they will likely tear you and your family apart. You need to consider what your limits are. How far are you willing to push your goals onto your family? For example, if you want to travel the world but have limited funds and three children, it would be wise to take this goal off of your short-term list and move it to your long-term list. Can you show support to your family if you are always gone? Can your twelve-year-old play soccer if you are taking guitar lessons? Can you have a good relationship with your wife if you are always working late? Try to stay open-minded when you evaluate these comparisons. Be as honest with yourself and family situation as possible.

4. Make goals that align with those of your loved ones. Eliminate or modify anything that creates distance or friction among you and your loved ones, and add goals that allow you and your family to improve, enjoy, live, and attain happily *ever after*. It's possible you have the time and money to learn guitar and support your twelve-year-old at the same time. Or maybe, instead of traveling the world by yourself, you can save up, pick one favorite destination, and take your family with you to that destination. It is important you find ways to reconcile the many desires and goals in your home.

Doing this exercise will allow you to have a greater understanding of your family's happiness as well as your own happiness, and will help your family to be successful.

My good friends the Coopers have discussed their goals for their life and family many times because their *ever after* is always changing and their respective goals for their own life are not the same as their spouse's goals. They had to decide if hunting, children, rock climbing, and backpacking could all fit into their life at the same time, or if any of these activities could fit at all. They altered their lists and goals so they could "fulfill each other's dreams." They take a camping trailer when they go hunting so everyone can come along. Since long backpacking trips are difficult with children, they purchased a comfortable backpack carrier so they could take their daughter on short hikes with them instead. The Coopers are enjoying life and fulfilling their goals.

If we have goals and objectives and work together as a family, we, like the Cooper family, can still be happy. We don't have to give up everything; sometimes, we just have to find a better way. Elbert Hubbard, a goal-setting expert, teaches that people do not succeed because they aren't smart enough or strong enough, but because they are not focusing their strengths around an objective (Hubbard, 2013). If we want to succeed and find happiness in our family life, we need to have goals and objectives that include and encompass our family.

Altered Reality

Every now and then, when I am feeling down, overwhelmed, unaccomplished, or ignored, deceptive thoughts lurk in my mind: things like, "I should have waited longer to get married," or "I could have earned my master's degree and had a thrilling career," or even "I would have such an easier life if I had decided not to have kids." This self talk sounds just as sad and detrimental as it really is. It is so easy to convince ourselves that another life choice would have made our *ever after* so much happier. When we indulge this type of thinking, we are succumbing to pure deception. No one is happy with everything in his or her life all the time. We are not missing out on a secret key to happiness that others discovered long ago. In fact, can you name one person you know that is one hundred percent happy one hundred percent of the time? My sister-in-law stated it eloquently when she said, "If you're waiting for something better to come along, you'll always be waiting."

Although we might want to see all the possible *ever afters* and alternate endings, it is impossible for us to see what doesn't exist. In reality, there is no "what if." You already made the choice to get on the ride, get married, and begin a family based on the information and feelings you had at the time. It is easy to see "superior paths" in retrospect, but how do you know those "superior paths" are really any better? Sometimes, we create alternate realities and lifestyles in our minds that are so much more appealing than the one we have. It is like crafting a whole new life in a video game, where your normally slightly heavy body is able to be trim and sexy, your penny-pinching self can live in a mansion, your kids can be educated at the finest schools, and your husband can do everything on your honey-do list. Whether we make up this alternate life in a game or in our minds, it is not real; it is a deception. Look at who you really are and what you really have, then choose to make your real life with your real family really wonderful.

I can't count the numerous times I have deceived myself by saying or thinking, "I have given up everything for my spouse and children." One particularly pathetic day, as I was moping over the hefty sacrifices I had made to have a family, I had an epiphany. In a life changing moment, I realized I didn't give up everything; I simply made the choice to let one dream go in pursuit of a better dream, a dream I wanted more. That dream was my family. I realized that if I had not had my children, I would have been lonely and longing for children. If I had pursued a master's degree or my dream career, I would be in major debt, missing my unborn children. I realized that day that I was definitely on the greener side of the mountain. We can't possibly chase every exciting pathway we find. We have to choose, and I'm guessing that, like me, you chose to pursue the dream of happily *ever after*. So instead of dwelling on our old and still unfulfilled dreams of sanity, exciting careers, freedom, travel, and so forth, we should work on making our current dream, the dream we chose, sensational.

The Dangers of Being Content

Not only are we deceived by our perceptions of events, but we are also deceived by our comfortable, and often deceptive interpretations of what it takes to have what we want. Sydney Harris, an American Journalist, was wise when he taught that people understand that they must work hard to be successful in any occupation, but feel entitled to have success in marriage without doing anything (Harris, 2013). The idea that we can do the bare minimum in our homes and with our families, and expect to have domestic harmony has become a plague of deception in our society. With all of the demands on our time and all of the expectations of family, friends, and society, we convince ourselves we will be happy and have a happy family if we do just enough to make it through the day. We are not intentional about our love and often don't put forth any extra effort or save time or energy for the ones we love. When we go to work or volunteer, we give our all, but when we get home, we allow ourselves to think the work we have already accomplished is sufficient, and we become convinced we are done for the day. We believe we can have a happy family by simply being with them, but here we are deceived. We are not going to have great family relations and a fabulous family life by simply getting by. We cannot obtain something marvelous by giving less than a marvelous effort.

A family life of just getting by is a life that yells out, "You are not worth the date, the flowers, the kiss, the compliment, or the time." People are precious and often very fragile. Give them love; show them you care about them by being intentional with family time and by planning and working as hard for them as you do for your boss, your friends, or your social organizations.

So many families find themselves discontent with their home, children, and spouse. There is great irony in this. We often say we don't have enough time for family, even though we watch TV instead of playing with the kids, or play the Xbox when we could be on a family outing. How much time do we spend on the computer when we could be on a date with our spouse? Are we chatting online with friends when we could be chatting with the real people who are begging for our attention in the room around us? As alluring as these virtual and distracting activities are, we won't find lifelong satisfaction and happiness in them. Happiness in family life is found by being intentional, working hard, and sacrificing. It is not found simply by getting by.

Life's Not Fair

When the doctors discovered that I had a heart arrhythmia and that I was very symptomatic, they reminded me that exercising or lifting children (or lifting anything for that matter) was very dangerous. They prescribed bed rest until the symptoms subsided. With very little forewarning, I found myself not able to do anything, pulling only about five percent of my usual load, while my husband and other family members pulled the other ninety-five percent.

We can't afford to be deceived by the myth that marriages and family leadership are based on a fifty-fifty work load, where each partner does their half of the labor. The reality is that most of the time it is a thirty-seventy or forty-sixty relationship. Sometimes it will be your husband pulling thirty percent and sometimes it will be you. There are even rare and beautiful moments when both partners can contribute their full hundred percent. Enjoy those times. Be productive and use them wisely. Sometimes work, illness, stress, and unforeseen events slow us down. Be patient with your spouse when you are giving ninety and they are giving ten; hopefully it won't be this way forever, and they will be so grateful to you for your extra efforts.

Don't let inaccurate or negative perceptions, selfishness, what-ifs, or an unfair workload pull you away from your dreams of happily *ever after*. If you find yourself wrapped up in the media's version of *ever after*, where magic wands flash and life is suddenly perfect and falling in love continues forever, come back to reality. Throw out this deception and align your goals to that which brings the most joy. Find happiness in the life you have by showing love to the ones you love the most. There are so many good things fighting for our attention, but don't let them deceive you. There is nothing more important than your family. Jobs come and go, school comes and goes, cars come and go, beauty comes and goes, but your family, whatever your relationship, will always be your family.

CHAPTER FOUR

Defining What's Important

Challenge: Do something with your spouse or children that is important to them

With one arm holding the phone, I rushed around the kitchen wiping off counters, stacking dishes in the dishwasher, and browning meat for dinner. I was talking with my mom about financial woes, injuries, the deadline for this book, doctor visits, and new school clothes, when she pointed out to me, "When you get to be my age, you look back on your life and realize that so much of what you thought was a big deal, didn't really matter at all."

The wisest people in my life are always telling me to take pictures, write down the funny things your kids say, spend more time with your kids, go on dates, have more sex, or take a vacation. No one ever tells me to have a cleaner house, worry more about finances, or buy the kids more new clothes because they know in the end those things are just not a big deal and that they are not what create happily *ever afters.*

So what are the important things in family life that need our strength and energy? Experience has shown me it is important to show interest in your loved ones' interests and show them they are more important than broken dishes, missed appointments, careers, or hobbies. It is important to support and lift up your loved ones in their needs and desires. It is also essential to be honest, reliable, and forgiving towards your family. It is critical to use your time for what provides long-lasting satisfaction—family.

Showing Interest

I love it when my husband helps me with my creative projects, and he loves it when I go fishing with him. Neither of us loves the other's hobby, but we love each other. We love making each other happy and we love being together. In order to show our loved ones that what is important to them is important to us, we must actually know what is important to them. I know it is important to my four-year-old to read her stories. I know it is important to listen to my nine-year-old and help her with creative projects. If we want to know what is important to our loved ones, it is important to pay attention, listen, and inquire. Sometimes, that means we have to stop doing what we are doing and refocus our attention on our family.

Once we figure out what is important to our family, we can take action. We have to get brave and creep out of our comfort zone. Go to the ball game or learn the rules of football. Bake a cake together, build a bookshelf, play pirates, do an art project, or dance in the living room like there is no tomorrow. There is no togetherness in families that are always doing their own thing separate from one another. Quell the temptation to stay safe in your zone by doing something with your loved ones that they love.

James, my brother and father of four boys, says, "I'm not a scouter. I haven't been one since I was ten years old, and I actually have a great treasure trove of negative experiences, emotions, and memories to draw on to remind me why I don't love scouting. Unfortunately, I'm the lucky father of four boys, and the ones who have experienced it *love* it. They love camping, hiking, biking, building, gaming, campfire-ing, and scouting in all its forms. I've slowly come to realize that while scouting can be great by itself, it's much more effective, exciting, and enjoyable when boys can do it with their dads. In fact, only a handful of the scouts in the boys' den even get that opportunity, coming mostly from single or uninvolved-parent homes, so I want to make sure my boys don't miss out on the great joy that can come by doing these things together. I've attended meetings, helped them build, tolerated den leaders, stood up to misinformed authorities, gone to day camp three years in a row (so far) and had generally great memories with my sons. I still don't like the scouting, particularly, and I probably never will, but my sons will, and I'll be next to them while they do."

It is exciting when someone is interested in you, your hobbies, and your passions. It is even better when that someone who is interested is someone you love. Don't blow off your family's concerns or joys just because they seem unimportant to you. They are important to them. Life is made up of thousands of seemingly menial things that make up who we are, who we become, and what we believe. Our attitude toward the important things in our loved ones' lives determines whether or not they feel loved and supported by us.

When I was seventeen years old, I had my sights set on a cutie. His family was moving, I was heartbroken, and after my final goodbyes to him, I went home. When I walked through the door, my mother was standing there with her arms open. She knew where I had been and what I had been doing. I buried my head in her shoulders and cried like a baby. She just held me. She didn't make fun of my teenage emotions. She didn't tell me to get over it; she cried with me. This was just a small moment in my life's history, but it made a big difference to me. I knew my parents were looking out for me. I knew they cared about what I cared about and how I felt.

My husband's aunt and uncle recently shared their experience of how, at the slightest show of dust or grime on her clothes, their three-year-old, Emma, would fall to pieces. She would play all day in the mud and dirt and be fine until her gaze crossed over the brown smear on her clothes, and then came the frantic screaming and crying. One evening, with all the family gathered at the dinner table, little Emma spilled a dot of ketchup on her shirt. As her father read the panic in her eyes, he immediately spilled food on his shirt. Her mother and siblings all followed suit. They knew it was important to her to look clean, and they also knew as a three-year-old she would always be dirty. Emma was quickly soothed when she realized it was okay to get a little messy, and she found great entertainment watching her entire family sacrifice their cleanly comforts to show they cared about her. It didn't matter to the family if Emma got dirty, but they knew it mattered to her, so they took action.

The next time your kids' toys break, show them your love. When they have girl or boy drama, listen. Be compassionate. When your spouse or child wins an award or gets a promotion, celebrate with them. Rejoice in their success. Go to your children's recitals and ball games. This support is important, and it becomes important to you because it is important to them.

Support

The gumball necklaces were a dazzling success at my sister's candy themed bridal shower. My dedicated husband pushed a drill bit through ten pounds of variegated pastel gumballs. This 3:00 a.m. ordeal was no small feat. He squeezed his manly hands into latex gloves, sanitized his itty-bitty tool bit, and found himself swathed in gumball dust. It was a mind-numbing task about which he could not have cared less, but he knew this party was special to me. Instead of laying his head on a pillow (which would have been my first instinct) or working on new electronic apps (which he loves to do), he drilled holes in gumballs. He later related that he felt invested and proud of the outcome, and I felt supported when he used his time and energy to help me in something that was important to me. He could have just wished me "good luck," but he didn't; he put aside things he wanted to do and helped me accomplish what I needed to do.

My husband was elated when he was finally able to start his own business. In his eyes, all of his dreams were coming true and his hard work was finally paying off. In my eyes, all of my dreams were on hold and the hard work was just beginning. He kept saying things like, "It is so exciting to have our own business," to which I would reply, often with a twang of bitterness, "This isn't my business. This is your dream, not mine. Good luck. I hope it works out so we can pay the mortgage." I was excited for him but I was not interested in helping him. Instead of being his cheerleader, I became the incessant rain on his parade. I wanted him to succeed, but mostly because I wanted to buy the kids nice Christmas presents and pay off the car. I didn't stop him from doing what he wanted to do, but I didn't actively help him, either. This was not support.

Support is a verb. It is an action. Simply saying, "Sure son, I think going out for cross country is a great idea," is not support. It takes time, energy, and effort to support someone. Sometimes it means you leave work early to watch that cross country meet or go running with your son to help him with his endurance. Maybe it means you teach an extra piano lesson or work a little over time to help pay for the extra expenses. Maybe it means helping your husband with the bookwork and acting as impromptu secretary while he gets his business on its feet. We didn't hop into our roller coaster cart with our one and only true love so that we could spend the rest of the ride pursuing our dreams alone.

People are More Important than Things

"Mom, Mom, Mom . . . it broke everywhere!"

Despite the urgency in the voice, I only waddled inside, in that oh-so-uncomfortable pregnant way. My husband was out of town and the first snow was coming. I was trying to clean the junk off the lawn, rake the leaves, and unhook the hose. As I approached the scene my child had warned me about, I could see a broken jar of peaches shattered across the entire kitchen floor. Not awesome! My first thought was probably not appropriate for sharing. My second thought was to get everyone away from the scattered shards of broken glass and keep them safe. My third thought was, "It is just a jar of peaches, why am I so upset?" My kids certainly didn't mean to drop the peaches, and in their hunger, due to my obvious lack of attention, they took things into their own hands. It just didn't end the sweet way they thought it would. In that moment, I remembered what my mom had said to me over and over: "*People are more important than things!*" As I wiped up the sticky juices and swept the shattered glass, I was determined to heed my mother's wisdom. I refrained from speaking the sharp words I had meant to say to my children, and apologized for ignoring them when they needed me. I helped the kids make lunch and then resumed my outdoor tasks. It was a good reminder that my children are more important than a broken jar of peaches or dead leaves on the lawn.

My friend Cherise recalls, "At probably ten years old, I was assigned to clean and organize the bottom cabinets in the kitchen. As I did so, I chipped a large knick in a glass candy dish that my parents had received as a wedding gift fifteen years earlier. With tears in my eyes and guilt in my heart, I showed my mom what I had done. She simply thanked me for cleaning and organizing, said it was an old candy dish anyway and showed love and comfort to my guilt. She told me to throw it away. I kept that little candy dish for years—chip and all—as a reminder that I was more important to my mom than a candy dish."

Just as Cherise knew she was more important to her mom than the candy dish, it is important for us to know that we are more important than anything else. Show your family through words and actions they are more important to you than objects, opportunities, or other people. They are more important than a great car, a great house, or a great career. They are more important than a boat or a new iPad. Stuff is just that—stuff. People, unlike stuff, feel deep emotion and are capable of incredible feats. Emotions that you elicit in others will create lasting memories, for good or bad. Instead of investing our time, money and emotions in things that will never change, laugh, love, or bring lasting joy, we should instead invest our time and energy in the ones we love.

When Jodi was six years old, she imagined herself as a secretary. Being the creative girl that she was, she equipped herself with a screwdriver "pen" and a piano bench "notepad." She was innocently enjoying her playtime, taking important memos and writing critical notes, when her mother discovered the scratches on the bench. As her mother screamed at her and began whipping her with the wet rag she was using to try to fix the scratches in the piano, Jodi recalled, "This was the moment in my life when I felt least loved." She knew at that moment, the piano bench was more important than Jodi was to her mom.

Every time my kids break a dish, my reading glasses, my great-grandma's vase, or the computer, I try to remind myself that my kids are more important than any of those objects. I am not condoning my children running around like crazy and ransacking everything of value because it's important to teach my children to be aware and take care of others' things as well as their own. When your children do slip up, let them know Great-grandma's vase was special and have them replace what they can, but more than anything, let them know how precious they are to you. It isn't worth destroying a child's innocent happiness and tender self-esteem or your own relationship with your spouse because someone destroyed an object or fumbled an opportunity.

Just One More Stop

"Just one more stop." These are the words I repeated to my children over and over. The kids worked hard in the yard picking up trash, mowing and weeding. We put up the pool and were excited to swim when the water was warmer. I informed them we had to go to the store first to get some sunscreen. Our quick run for sunscreen, however, turned into an expedition for a full list of necessities—diapers, wipes, and who knows what else. Our quick trip took longer than I or they had planned. On the way back, I told them we just had to make a stop at the library and return our overdue books. While at the store, a conscientious soul reminded me it was voting day and I should get to the polls before they closed. Not wanting to miss my opportunity to be a good citizen, and not wanting to take my children out again later, I told them, "Just one more stop," and off we went, only to find I was at the wrong building. My district voted in another place, so again I told my children, "Really this is the last stop." To my relief, it really was the last one, but it got me thinking, "How reliable am I?" It was 4:30 p.m. when my kids finally got in the pool, and we had started our work at 10:00 a. m. I want my children to trust me, but how can they if they can't count on me? How can they rely on me if I do not do what I say I will do?

Trust is important, and I take pride in being reliable with friends, neighbors, and especially work, but my family seems to be the group I can let slide. Of all people, my children and spouse should be able to rely on me in any circumstance. If I say I will be there, I should be there. No matter how tired I am or how many things I need to get done, it should be a top priority for me. If I say I'm going to do it, I need to do it. I think often we expect our families to be understanding of the things that pull us away from them, and I also think we as family members should try to be understanding of such situations, but relying on such mercies from our families should be the exception and not the rule.

I remember an evening when my husband said he would be home to watch the kids so I could go to work. He didn't make it and I will say I was so upset, and you can safely consider that an understatement. I felt like I should be able to rely on him and in that moment, I couldn't. It made me feel like his work, activities, and integrity were more important to him than my work, activities, and integrity. Don't worry, he knows I am writing this, and I have since forgiven him. I know my husband loves me and I knew that then, but we had a pretty in-depth conversation that evening. He reminded me that it was his boss holding him back and that he didn't let me down by choice. I told him that if I could count on him in general, then when things out of his control really did happen, it would be so much easier for me to be understanding of his predicament. In family life things do arise, and if your home is like mine, they arise more often than not. Sometimes we go to the wrong voting precinct, or, due to situations beyond our control, we must work late, but these situations should be the exception and not the rule. We should be the ones our families can count on, trust in, and rely on.

Tighten the Lug Nuts

My brother-in-law, Joe, a father of five, drove home from work. He was tired and anxious to get home to his exhausted wife. The finances were tight and he was deep in thought. As he flew south on the interstate, the car began to shake and make loud knocking noises. He pulled over to the side of the road to inspect the car and found nothing—no noises, no shaking. He got back in and kept driving. Two minutes later, driving at interstate speeds, his front tire fell off and rolled down the freeway. He struggled to maintain control of the car with only three wheels, and luckily made it to the shoulder safely. With his tire missing, he was stranded. Despite limited finances, he called a tow truck.

Two days prior to this, he had changed the brakes on his car and upon replacing the tire, had failed to tighten the lug nuts. Joe related his experience to me and said, "One small error, casually neglected, created a life threatening situation that caused hours of grief and financial strain." He compared this experience to his family, realizing that relationships have lug nuts that need to be carefully, consistently tightened and not casually overlooked or forgotten. Small things forgotten or avoided can have large, disastrous consequences.

For marriages and family, those lug nuts are the pillows on the ride of life that make the journey smoother and the bumps less noticeable. They are forgiveness (telling your husband you love him even when he let you down), compassion (crying with your heartbroken teenager), patience (holding your tongue when you hear the glass shatter), and humor (laughing when life is getting crazy). The lug nuts are saying "I love you," going on a date, really listening, showing affection, understanding, and giving your time. This father went on to say, "If you forget to tighten even one of those lug nuts, the integrity of your car is jeopardized. When you forget to tighten one of those relationship lug nuts, the integrity of your life or family is jeopardized. It is not a risk worth taking." Don't wait until your family vehicle is banging, sputtering, and threatening to fall to pieces. Don't wait for a crisis to motivate you to take action, or convince you of the necessity of living the Red Punch Experiment. It is going to hurt when your roller coaster car crashes and you realize you could have done something to prevent it.

I recently had a major fallout with my teeth; they were definitely in crisis mode. I had been neglecting my dental checkups, I flossed only occasionally, and I may have missed a few opportunities to brush before bed. My teeth were hurting long before I finally went to the dentist. Sadly, my neglect cost me dearly, both financially and physically, and it literally took me thousands of dollars and several long months to fix. It was incredibly painful and I quickly found myself regretting my lack of attention to my teeth.

Much like our marital and family relations, had I paid attention to what was important—annual checkups, flossing my teeth, and extra brushing—it would have been a far quicker, less painful, and more affordable fix. If we invest our time and efforts in the important things to our families, making small adjustments before we reach crisis mode, it will be far easier to maintain happy family life. Our fights will have quicker solutions, our love will be stronger, and we will spend less time regretting things we wish we had done differently. However, if we wait to spend time with our loved ones, do not support them, or are not reliable and trustworthy; the task of repairing our relationships will be extremely difficult, possibly painful, and certainly time consuming. It can mean the difference between simply filling a small cavity and having a root canal surgery—or the difference between a minor miscommunication and divorce papers.

When I get to be my mother's age, I don't want to be pondering my life and worrying over what might have been if I had paid attention to and acted on what was most important in my life. I want to know that I spent my efforts on what is most important: my family.

I know an honorable and very much in love older couple who experienced tragedy. The husband spent his life taking care of runaways, families in need, and others who needed his assistance. If you can name it, he probably did it. Despite the good he was doing, this placed a great deal of pressure on his wife as he left to serve others while leaving her to attend to their home and children. When she got sick, he realized how much she needed him, but he had waited too long. She had needed him long before her health had turned for the worse, and he missed the precious time he might have had with her. Although he spent his life doing good things, in the end as he laid her to rest, he lost what he valued most. Instead of letting her be the main attraction, his wife was his fallback. He didn't neglect her because he was out at the bar or hanging with his buddies. In his case, it was the good things that pulled him away from the best thing.

When we are young, it is easy to get wrapped up in a growing family or career, and we often neglect our most important priority—our spouse. My good friend Cherise shares, "My parents started their family right away. My mom was pregnant three days after their marriage. Between pregnancies, nursing, and demanding babies, my dad often felt like he never got my mom all to himself. She thought this was only a phase in their life and someday it would be over and they would have time together. Little did they know that cancer would take her dear life at the young age of forty-eight. One of her last words of advice that she shared with my then twenty-five and married sister was, that despite the business of raising kids and the lack of finances that she (my sister) was already dealing with, she should make her husband most important. She told her to go on dates, find sitters for weekend getaways, and strengthen your marriage. You never know when things aren't going to go as planned and you'll be looking back and wishing that you had spent more time with the one you love most."

At the beginning of your roller coaster ride, it is just you and your sweetheart. As your cart fills with children, careers, and other aspirations, don't lose sight of your spouse and your relationship with them. How could Cherise's mother know she would never go beyond the phase of motherhood or have the time to focus on her spouse as she had planned? We should all heed her counsel and spend more time with our one and only love. Put them first, and I doubt you will ever regret it.

I am always reminding my husband when we don't get our date night: "I didn't marry you to have kids or money, I married you because I wanted to be with *you*." My mother says, "Though your spouse cannot always take precedence, they should be your first priority." It is important to make your marriage and children your priority, and make sure they are never playing backup to your other priorities.

Forgiveness

Forgiveness is one of the cushions we should bring with us into marriage and it is vitally important in creating a happily *ever after*. Forgiveness alone can keep your car from derailing. It can soften the blow of any turn if you allow it to and it can keep you from stalling on the track. You could act on every important thing we have previously discussed in this chapter, but if you cannot forgive your spouse or children for the injustices they will inevitably throw your way, your happily *ever after* will likely be tainted with sadness and bitterness.

I was upset at my husband for years over that night he worked late and didn't come home in time for me to go to work. I still loved him, and for the most part we were happy, but what I thought of as his lack of concern for my integrity often ate at me. He had no idea I was even thinking about it, but I would replay that night over and over until I was fuming. Finally, I realized I had to let it go. He wasn't suffering over this, but I was, and it was hard to completely give my love to him when I felt such bitterness. In the end, this incident wasn't truly important, except for the fact that it was hurting my marriage. When I finally forgave him, I was able to refocus on the happy part of my *ever after* rather than my hurt pride. Apologizing is important, but it cannot compare to the power of forgiveness. My husband apologized right after the incident happened, but it wasn't until I decided to forgive him that the pain was gone.

A dear friend told me in tears of how her father had once had an affair resulting in a child. Her mother was obviously heartbroken and the children felt angry and betrayed. Her father was very sorry and, despite his unfaithfulness, wanted to remain with his wife. After counseling together, all of the children voted that their parents divorce immediately, all but one, that is. My friend was able to see beyond the moment's circumstance and was willing to attempt healing the broken relationships. She saw the pain her mother was experiencing, but she could also see how much the pain would be magnified with a divorce. She loved her father and wanted him to be with their family. Because of the love she had for everyone in her family, she saved her family. Even after such tragedy and dishonesty, the family triumphed. It wasn't easy to forgive such betrayal, and the decision they made may not be the right decision in every circumstance. It is important to note the family could have forgiven their father and still considered divorce. However, I use this experience because it illustrates the power of willing forgiveness. It was a difficult and indisputably long process, but that process provided healing and helped to begin rebuilding the foundation upon which the family stood. True love and happiness are built and sustained on a foundation of forgiveness, and such forgiveness provides unseen pathways through hurt and pain.

Kerry Egan, a hospice chaplain, wrote of her experience with those who were dying. She wrote of how they would tell her about their families, parents, spouses, and children. They would reminisce over memories of these people and the lessons they had learned about life and love. They were not interested or concerned with careers, theories, or doctrines. Their joys, sorrows, and ultimately their lives, revolved around their families (Egan, 2012). Our families are what are truly important. Our lives will not always be filled with work and business, and one day we will find we have plenty of time on our hands to ponder what has been and what should have been most important in our lives.

While attending a parent-teacher conference for my daughter, the teacher asked me if I felt the word problems on her math homework were too vague and confusing. I thought for a moment and confidently replied no. I felt like it was good practice for my daughter to learn how to pick out the pertinent information needed to solve the problem. While pondering this, I realized that in order to solve life's problems, we need to be able to decipher what is important in the theoretical whirlwinds distracting us at every turn.

The extra facts and numbers were alluring and confusing to my daughter because they seemed important, but as soon as she sleuthed out the right numbers, the rest was easy. Until we can focus on and find what is most important, we will not be able to obtain the happiness we desire. We must wade through the fields of excess and find the flowers that are covertly masked by the weeds. Only then will we find our equation for happily *ever after*.

As we coast or speed through our *ever afters*, we need to keep our priorities set on the most important things or we will surely find ourselves regretting such neglect later on. We have so much say in the happiness of our families and lives. We can enact the principles of the Red Punch Experiment every day as we place our families above possessions, and become reliable, supportive, and trustworthy to the people we love the most. We can show forgiveness no matter the crime. We shouldn't squander our opportunity for happiness because we don't put forth the effort to act on what is important.

CHAPTER FIVE

Tick-Tock

Challenge: Take time to do something fun with your spouse or family and also do one thing for yourself that you love

People Need Time

Every day on the drive home from my Daniel's kindergarten class, I would ask him how his day was. I always received a prompt "fine." I soon learned if I wanted to retrieve anything from my son's inquisitive mind about his life, his tender emotions, or his concerns, I was going to have to dig. I would rack my brain thinking of specific questions and would latch onto any response I was given. Still, I would find a serious lack of introspect into his curious mind and life. A few weeks into the year, I stumbled upon something miraculous.

Daniel and I were making cookies just for fun. They were chocolate chip, which is his favorite. I didn't do any probing or ask any questions but as the flour dust floated through the air, out of nowhere he began opening up to me. He told me between gooey chocolaty snitches that his recess football team kept losing and he had a crush on a girl and thought he might marry her, and then he told me about what he did at "centers" during school. We discovered that Daniel didn't actually know the rules of football or even really how to play football. We told him that he didn't need to worry about getting married until he was done with college, and learned his favorite part of centers was tracing dinosaurs.

I was floored at the buckets of information that had just been poured onto me, and an obvious realization hit me. If I want to know my kids and spouse—their problems and their lives—a two-minute conversation on the way home from school or a quick phone call, isn't going to suffice. When we analyze the things that are most important, it becomes apparent they all require our time.

If the only time I spend interacting with my husband is over dinner and in those half-awake minutes before bed, we start to feel distant from each other, we are less patient, and we pounce with aggression more frequently. When we go on a date, have a real human conversation, work happily together or take time to be intimate, that time draws us back together, and once again we find ourselves enjoying one another. Our quality time spent together helps us more fully understand each other's joys, fears, and frustrations. It enables us to continue creating a bond that goes far beyond problems with the kids and the overly treaded "there's not enough money left in the budget" conversation. Giving our time allows us the opportunity to take care of the things that are most important.

When our friends need something done, whether that be a pipe fixed, a lunch out to vent, or a little remodeling help, we jump to do it. When our kids need to talk or our spouse needs a break or some love, we often find ourselves saying, "Just a minute," "I don't have time right now," "I need to send some emails," "I have to finish the dishes," or "I have too much work." Somehow, our "just a minute" turns into an hour, the dishes turn into a project of cleaning the floors, and the work never ends.

When I let myself become waterlogged by the many tasks before me, never taking time to soak up the sun or the valuable people around me, tension and unhappiness flourish. In these dismal times, the trifling headaches and stiff muscles from the jolting of my roller coaster ride of life become inflamed, until they are throbbing and unable to be ignored. It is usually at this point that I become stressed to the max and unsatisfied with my *ever after*. When I play with my kids, watch a movie with my husband, or just spend time with my family doing what's important, the headaches dissipate and my reservoirs of love and happiness are filled, even if many of my daily tasks are left undone.

Valuing the Relationship

My life is a testament that I spend my time and energy on what I value most. Time flies when I am watching movies, designing wedding flowers, talking on the phone, or hiking in the mountains, because I consider these things important, valuable, enchanting, or relaxing. So I must ask myself, do I value my family, consider them important, or find them enchanting? Does time fly when we are at a soccer game, playing dolls with the kids, or listening to our spouse regurgitate their less than thrilling day? In many such moments, I often find myself feeling antsy, like I need to start on some more pressing or enthralling activity, whatever that may be. I catch my eyes darting around the perimeter of my home or whatever location I'm in, taking in the destruction, sounds, or people funneling around me. My thoughts are pulled away from what and who I should be valuing and spending time with. This attitude is not quality time, and I am not valuing the people I love.

We don't need to be fanatics about everything our family does, but we should show them we value them, and the best way to do that is by giving them focused quality time. Our families know when our time is invested in them and when it is invested elsewhere. We bend over backwards to be good hosts, friends, and co-workers, and all of those things take time. We would never dream of pushing such responsibilities away, but we will push away our own families, falling prey to the excuse that we just don't have time. We need to make time and train our brains to take pleasure in our families.

My sister Heather had sent her two daughters to bed, only to hear their murmured whispers long after they should have been sound asleep. She was drained and felt she had already dispensed her allotted time on her children for the day and was ready to instill order and obedience. As she approached their door, she shifted her plans. Instead of telling them to go to sleep, she sat down on their floor and asked them what they were talking about. Sheepishly, her daughters began to relate the conversation about the boys they had crushes on. When she got up twenty minutes later, she realized the time she had just given to her daughters was incredibly valued and valuable. She was stunned at their eagerness to share the personal and secret affairs of their lives, and hoped that her willingness to give her time showed that she cared. She also hoped that this experience would help them to trust her later on when such relationships with boys could hold greater consequences in their lives.

We should allot as much time to our families as we can. Sometimes it will be inconvenient and sometimes it will interfere with other plans, but in the end we won't have to regret that we spent our time in the pursuit of less important things.

Time Priority Analysis

Look back at the last week of your life and do a time priority analysis. If you can't remember that far back, look at the last twenty-four hours and make an hour-by-hour list of what you did and where you spent your time. When you have completed your list, categorize it, starting at the top with what you spent the most time on to the bottom with what you spent the least amount of time on. With your list in hand, answer the following questions.

1. Did you put housework or your career before your children and spouse?

2. Did you make uninterrupted time to talk with your children and spouse?

3. Did you do something fun with your kids?

4. Have you eased the burden of a friend but neglected the burdens of your spouse?

5. Did you go on a date with your spouse?

6. Did you attend any of your children's or spouse's extracurricular activities?

7. Did you spend time serving your loved ones or easing their burdens?

8. Were you intentional about the time you spent with your family?

9. Did you take any time for yourself?

10. Did you spend time watching television, surfing the web, Tweeting, playing online games, or keeping up on Facebook?

Now that you have a better understanding of where you are spending your time, honestly evaluate how you could give more time to your family and then make yourself a schedule for the next day or week and stick to it. We need to fit our family into our busy lives.

Time is of the Essence

Time is an opportunity to plan, to be with the ones we love, to change old ways and discover better ways. It is an occasion to cherish what we adore, create amazing experiences, and build bonds meant to last forever. Time is a constant window of opportunity to live our happily *ever after*. We can better utilize such a limited resource by finding ways to enjoy the monotony of work and by being intentional in our play and relaxation. By doing this, we will make our time with our family more meaningful.

Work

I spend excess amounts of my time and energy trying to convince my children that most of life will be consumed with the adventures we refer to as work, and that that's okay. I have yet to convert them, but either way, the principle is sound. Much of our family time is spent working, which should in no way be considered a negative thing. Work provides wonderful opportunity, if we let it, to laugh together, talk together, and make memories together. It allows us to learn and teach new skills, do hard things, and to build confidence in family members and ourselves.

If we approach work with the wrong focus, however, it can be a rotten family ordeal. When we perceive work as a negative entity only to be gotten rid of and out of the way as quickly as possible, we are focusing only on the end product. Sometimes we focus so much on the finish line that we become irritated at anything hindering our progress, whether that be a lack of knowledge, a butterfly, disorganization, a phone call, or children in general.

When we remodeled our house, we wanted our children to be involved. So we made it a point not to be upset or feel inconvenienced by their inconvenient handiwork. As our son poked unnecessary peep-holes in the sheet rock with the drill, our daughter filled them in with mud, and I followed by scraping off the globs of excess. Our son, who was two at the time, used his artistic creativity to splatter our walls with freshly-painted handprints. The remodel took longer than we had anticipated as we had to do a little more painting and touch up work, but the extra time spent was worth it and the memories are precious. Not all of our work experiences are this successful, but moments like these motivate me to be a little more thoughtful, a little more creative, and much more patient.

In a questionable moment of parenting, I caved like a washed out mine, and told my kids they could have their long-desired kitty if they could keep their rooms clean, beds made, and trash out for thirty days. I knew they would never do it because they hate cleaning their rooms. However, to my utter disappointment and displeasure, cleaning their rooms became a sudden adventure to be mostly enjoyed. Instead of moaning about the strewn books, mountains of Legos, and heaps of clothing lying next to the tipped laundry basket, they dreamed about their new cat, thinking of names and making feeding schedules. Suddenly, the work they were sure would take a lifetime was completed in a flash, without any tears or threats. The work was fun. My kids can scrape poop out of the kitty litter and enjoy it as long as we make it fun. Work will always be prevalent. In fact it will likely fill most of our time. I can't think of a better reason to make it enjoyable.

What Happened to Fun?

It is crucial that we are intentional about playtime or it will shrivel and evaporate itself right out of our family life. If we make plans to go to the zoo, it happens. If we say, "maybe if we have time or money we'll go to the zoo," it never happens. Playtime is the pot at the end of the rainbow. It gives us a change of pace and something to look forward to. Sometimes I find myself dreading any extra activity that impedes my sleep, but after I actually get out and do something fun, I am happier. I feel less weighed down by life and more carefree. I find it so much easier to see the happy in my *ever after* when I take time to simply enjoy my *ever after*.

It is fun to play with the kids at the park and give them never-ending underdogs. It is fun to take them to the pool and teach them how to swim. It is fun to feed the ducks and be chased by the geese, and it is fun to dance in the rain and rock out to the closing credits at the movies. It is fun to go shopping or to the fair. I saw a billboard a few years ago that said, "Remember fun . . . it still is." Don't stop loving life and doing fun things just because times are hard. Those are the moments we need joy the most.

When we play together, we remember it and usually those memories are recalled with fondness. Playtime makes people feel loved because it is happy time, free of stress, that is spent together. It is the perfect time to make memories. Every fourth of July, we take our kids to the annual Freedom Festival. The kids, through the art of face paint, transform into super heroes, butterflies, and princesses. We slowly turn cherry red as the heat of the sun melts away our sunscreen, and the raspberry juice from our snow cones drips down the kid's dirt stained faces. Everyone gets a small sum to purchase something from the oh-so-alluring booths, and even if we wanted to stay away, we couldn't. We are always refreshed as we gulp our Texas Twister, the ultimate lemonade to quench our thirst. Everyone enjoys the festival and looks forward to it. It is our playtime tradition and memory maker.

Create time you can always look forward to through traditions. Family traditions are the peanut butter and honey that bind families together. Dr. William J. Doherty teaches that traditions bring unity and attribute to a sense of belonging to something special (Doherty, 1999). My father said, "Traditions are very important to family play time. Some families have set vacations they take every year to a lake house or resort or camping at a favorite spot. However, the venue really doesn't matter; what really matters is the time spent and memories created."

One of my favorite traditions is eating dinner together as a family each night. I look forward to this time as a fun time, not because I love cooking or doing dishes, but because it is often the only time in the day our entire family is together. Each night, I ask every person at the table what their favorite part of the day was. I learn oodles about their friends, school, work, and concerns, and about the funny things that happen. Amidst the chaos, there is laughter and love.

Couples that Play Together Stay Together

After the birth of our second child, in the mist of busy work and school schedules, my husband and I were feeling smothered by our increased loads and in need of some alone time. Following in the footsteps of my wise and long-wed parents, we had a weekend date. It was the first time I had left my kids with a sitter overnight and I quickly discovered my attachment issues. As we bid farewell, my husband had to lug me away as I spewed the last of my instructions. I felt like I was abandoning my newly hatched eggs on the sands of a beach somewhere to be devoured by birds. An hour out, I was still fluttering with anxiety. By the time we got to the hotel in Park City, I was just beginning to relax.

By the next morning, I decided the pelicans could munch on my eggs for a while, and I was converted to the overnighter. My husband and I still reminisce about this particular trip. It rejuvenated us as a couple and became a marriage saving tradition. On our night away, we loved having uninterrupted romance whenever we wanted, trying new foods and stores, and simply enjoying one another. When we were away from the kids, I got to be Michelle, not Mom, and it made me feel like a new woman. We came home loving each other and appreciating each other so much more because we spent time enjoying one another. Long hours and high demands take their toll on relationships, and the only way to stick together is to spend time together.

A good friend told me about her in-laws and some of the struggles they faced in their marriage. They had seven kids under the age of fourteen when one of their children was in a horse accident that rendered him mentally handicapped. Such a trial could easily destroy a marriage, but they are still happily married many years later. They attribute their "saved" marriage to having a date once a week, a night away once a month, and a getaway for a week once a year. This is a marriage saving tradition.

Family traditions, vacations, and memories are important, but one day the kids will move out and you and your spouse will be left with only each other. Your most important relationship is that of husband and wife. Give it time, and keep sweeping your one and only off their feet and having traditions, vacations, and memories with just the two of you. When you begin mumbling under your breath about how your husband doesn't get it, and your wife doesn't appreciate you, it is time to play. Leave work, kids, and bills at home. After enjoying the memories of many family vacations and weekend dates with his sweetheart, my dad said it perfectly: "I guess the more I think about family vacations and traditions, the more I realize how important they have been in my life."

Relax

After driving her husband to work because their other car was in the shop, my friend Gina stopped at the store to get the snack for her son's soccer team, picked up her son, and ran him to his scrimmage game. She raced home, only to play chauffer again to her daughter who was going to summer camp. On her way out, she spotted the mechanic driving by to drop off her newly repaired car. She hollered out the window, "I'll be back in ten and I'll give you a check." As they passed Subway, her daughter told her to stop and pick up a sandwich, but Gina reminded her that the mechanic was waiting. Her daughter pointed out that she needed to eat before leaving to camp. Needless to say, her daughter won.

Gina dropped off her daughter with the youth leaders and impatiently unloaded her daughter's gear on the lawn. After breaking away from a talkative camp leader, and scolding her son for wiping blobs of boogers that looked like garden snails down the backseat of her new car, Gina drove home hastily. After paying her uber-patient mechanic, she packed the other kids back in the car and went to pick up her other son from his scrimmage. She took the kids home for a lunch of reheated leftovers, and put together a meal for Grandpa. She began to herd the kids back to the car with unfulfilled hopes of getting the house picked up, but her son refused to budge. He didn't want to run around anymore. After some serious coercion, they were on the road again to pick up the hubby from work. They arrived late, and immediately jetted to Grandpa's to give him dinner and help with yard work. As Murphy's Law would have it, time with Grandpa took far longer than planned and Gina missed an important phone call from her doctor. When Gina's husband asked what was for dinner, bitter silence settled between Gina and her husband for the remaining ride home. She was done. The kind of done where you lock yourself in your room, speak to no one, and mope with your chocolate as tears trickle down your tired cheeks.

When Gina told me this story, I couldn't help but laugh, to which she replied, "I didn't think it was that funny." After writing down her day in her journal she called me, and said she still didn't think it was that funny but she could understand why I would laugh. She reread the un-exaggerated charade of her day and said, "If this was a friend telling me about their day I would say, 'Honey, I know how to fix your problem. First, eat some breakfast; take a shower, sit down, and slow down, do something—anything—for yourself.'

Gina needed to take time to relax. She was taking care of everyone else but neglecting herself. Before taking off in any airplane, you will hear the flight attendant say something like, "Put on your own mask before assisting others." There is a very obvious reason for this advice. If we try to get our child's mask on first and pass out in the process, we may die before helping our child, who will then also die. If, however, we take this practical and lifesaving advice, we will save two lives. So it goes in life. When we get singed and burned out because we always go, go, go, not only are we going to lose the life in ourselves, but our family will feel the effects of our strain as well.

Our body, mind, spirit, and brain need repose. If we are not given this repose, we will quickly find ourselves with a depleted crater that was meant to be our much-needed reservoir. In any relationship, sacrifice must be made. If you never take care of yourself, you won't have anything left to sacrifice. Build your reserve through relaxation and allow your family to do the same. For me, relaxation is found in walking peacefully near the apple orchards, mentally savoring the delicious photos in my favorite food magazine, or penning my life's work in my journal. Maybe relaxing to you is enjoying a quiet cup of tea, or maybe it's mountain biking, carpentry, interior design, or baking. Whatever it is that soothes your soul and fills your reserves, make time to do it. As long as you are living, the work will never be done, so, like play time, you must be intentional about relaxation time.

One evening, when my husband was out of town, we were chatting over the phone. It was around 10:00 p.m. He was getting ready for bed, and I told him I was going to fold laundry. "Man," he said, "you have a tough boss." It took me by surprise. I am pretty tough on myself. I was tired, I was sick, and I had been working all day. I love work—I always have—but I was fast becoming my own worst boss. I would never expect someone else to stay up all night folding laundry. Instead, I would tell them to relax, read a book, or enjoy their family because the laundry would get folded . . . eventually. But for myself, I was demanding overtime every single day.

How can we show love to our family if we become so tired and so hardened that we have no love left to give? How can we enjoy the ride of our life when we are too tired to take in the scenery? We can't lock ourselves in our room every day, gorging ourselves with spoonfuls of Nutella, as delicious as that sounds, and live happily *ever after*. To be happy, we need to find joy in the work we do, play and make memories with our family, and give ourselves and loved ones time to relax and enjoy the ride we call life.

Only Twenty-Four Hours

After months of aggravation trying to smash the idea of work before play into our children's stubborn craniums, my husband came up with the perfect lesson. He rummaged up a bucket of rocks, which represented the things, or work, that had to be done in a day. For our children that meant going to school, doing homework, cleaning out the dishwasher, picking up floors, brushing their teeth, and so forth. He also had a bucket of sand, which represented play time or free time. He put an empty jar in front of them and tagged it as the twenty-four hours we have in a day. He asked the kids what they wanted to do first, work or play. Of course they wanted to play. So he poured the sand into the twenty-four hour jar. Then he had the kids put the rocks (work) into the jar. The rocks were obviously not going to fit. My husband dumped it out and put the work (rocks) into the jar first, followed by the play (sand). To our children's awe, it all fit snugly in the jar.

Family life is a lot like this sand and rock analogy. If our family is our priority and is the first thing to go into the jar—if we take time with them, make them breakfast, rub their shoulders, play a game with them, or listen to them—when the end of the day comes, they will not be forgotten. Maybe it is as simple as planning your husband's favorite meal or calling your wife on your lunch break to see how she is doing. Maybe it is rescheduling a meeting to make it to your son's football game. If, however, we wait until all of our other tasks are checked off, we will find family rarely fits into our twenty-four hour day.

My younger brother Justin said, "Growing up my father was a busy man, a busyness that grew as I got older. His full schedule was largely due to growing work responsibilities. His commitment to work was strong. However, I always knew that his family was first, and that I was important and worth his time. The time he spent supporting me left an indelible impression on me that impacts me now as a father. Throughout high school, I was involved in sports year-round, as well as [in] choir and other extracurricular activities. There is not one event that I can think of that my father was not in attendance [at]. I'm sure there were a few, but I know that he made it a priority to be there. I remember the last track race I ever ran. The memory does not stick because I did particularly well or anything else specifically associated with the sport or outcome. I remember that race because there was only one voice I heard while I ran. My father had positioned himself on the last turn of the track, right where he knew I made my move, the move that would determine the race for me. As I neared the turn, I heard a very clear voice cheering me on with the greatest vigor I had ever heard. It was my father. I knew that he was there for me. He was there because he loved me. He was there because it was important to me. I'm sure there was work he needed to be doing for his job or house projects that needed to be done. But he put everything else aside, stood on that turn, and cheered his son on. Now, almost ten years later, I remember this experience of a father's love and dedication with great fondness."

Justin's dad made time for him even with an overwhelming schedule because his dad valued him, enjoyed him, and wanted him to be happy. Years later, instead of regret, both father and son find joy and satisfaction in the valuable relationship that has been created because Justin's father spent his time on what mattered most. He filled his jar with the most important things first. Our families are the reason accomplishing anything is really worthwhile. Put them in your jar first.

Use your Time for that which Satisfies

Time and money are a driving force for most of us. Both are a valuable and limited resource, and depletion of either causes stress. Neither can be retrieved once they are gone. We make it a point to use these commodities in the wisest and most fulfilling way possible. No one is going to buy a shirt they hate and be happy they spent money on it. That would be as useful as knowing you need to exercise but sitting on the couch next to the treadmill feeling fat and tired instead. Suddenly, the time for exercise is up and you still feel like you and the couch have morphed into eternal mates.

It is the same with your family. We can't get the time we have with them back. My husband and I were discussing family when I realized, "We will never just have time with the family. If we want to be with our family we have to choose to be with them." We should make choices with our time and resources that will allow us to feel satisfied, knowing we have spent our time on that which is most worthwhile.

There are many nights I have been so exhausted. Every part of me has wanted to just lie down and relax. I haven't wanted to read stories to the kids, cuddle with the spouse, go to another soccer game or piano recital, or write in my journal. I have wanted to be left alone, but something inside me has persisted in telling me this respite from my family would not bring happiness. I always have a tendency to fight with myself in these moments, right up until the point I get off the couch and do what I know I should be doing already. Your family is precious. Don't lose what is most important to you by spending your time and efforts for things that bring no lasting joy or satisfaction.

CHAPTER SIX

Our Family through Our Eyes

*Challenge: Give a thoughtful and sincere compliment
to each member of your family*

Self-Personification and Self-Fulfilling Prophecy

When my oldest daughter was born, I made a resolution that when she made me upset I wouldn't say anything negative about her. For instance, instead of saying, "She is such a brat," or "She is so mean," I would just tell her she was silly. When she was about three, after doing something that annoyed me, I repeated, "You are so silly." In a huff she replied, "Why do you always tell me I'm silly? I don't want to be silly!"

It is interesting that my daughter felt like she had to become the kind of person I told her she was. People naturally tend to become who they believe they are, and they often believe what others tell them they are. This is explained through what is called self-personification and self-fulfilling prophecy. Self-personification is when a person's character or traits become what they previously believed or visualized them to be. This is influenced by self-fulfilling prophecy, a theory coined by sociologist Robert K Merton, who explains it as believing something to be true that isn't initially true, so that eventually we act on that falsehood until it becomes factual (Merton, 1968).

My daughter wasn't actually being silly, but because I told her she was silly, it made her feel like she needed to be. If I tell my husband he is lazy enough times, there is a good chance he is going to act lazy because he has heard it so many times he believes that he really must be, or might as well be. If I tell my child she is stupid enough times, she may believe it. Whether what I say about her is true or not, the likelihood of that prediction becoming true increases because my child will increasingly perceive herself as stupid and begin to act on those perceptions.

This concept can produce positive outcomes just as well as it can produce negative ones. If I tell my husband I love him, the odds of him feeling loved, acting loved, and popping in with a lush bouquet of Gerbera daisies will increase. If I tell my children they are fun, they will be more apt to up their fun factor. If I praise my children's creativity enough times, they will soon be putting good use to my old and broken appliances in an attempt to invent the latest version of the iPad. This subtle technique, when used positively, will help our families grow and succeed.

So what does this concept have to do with having a happily *ever after*? The more you cheer for your family and tell them they can do it, the better people they are likely to become. The more wonderfully you treat them, the more convinced they are of their wonderfulness. The more they believe they are wonderful, the more you will believe it, and the more perfect your perception of them and your *ever after* will become. My husband wisely stated, "You will see them for what they are and can be, rather than what they aren't and won't aspire to become."

"It's Not What You Say, but How You Say It"

Every interaction with our loved ones involves communication in one form or another. It is impossible not to communicate; even when you refrain from speaking, you are still communicating. Hence, the way we choose to communicate with our families is important. The old saying holds true—it's not what you say, but how you say it. Sometimes we have to tell our children they've done something that needs to be corrected, or point out a glaring weakness to our spouse, but we do not need to be mean, belittling, or critical in order to address our concern. This is especially valid with our spouse, as they should be considered our equal. It is possible to instill positive personification *and* teach or discuss difficult matters at the same time.

I was rushing the kids from the grocery store to my car in my usual frenzied and late manner, and as I buckled my sweet Julia into her seat, I found candy I had not purchased. My three-year-old daughter wanted a sugary treat from the store and innocently took it and put it in her pocket. I think almost all of my children, and probably most of your children, have done something similar. I knew right away that my child wasn't being defiant, but that she had just seen something she wanted and grabbed it. She tried to do what she sees me do. I go to the store, put things in my basket, and take them home. She simply didn't understand the part where I pay for it.

Instead of yelling at her and labeling her as a lost and hardened criminal at the age of three, I talked to her about taking things that were not hers, and discussed why that was wrong. I told her she was not a bad girl, but she had stolen something, and that was wrong. I could have made a scene, yelled at her, and left her feeling like she would never reach her potential, but that was not the lesson I wanted to instill. I wanted to teach her to be honest, not convince her she was dishonest. Since that time, my daughter has not stolen from the store and I have never worried about her being a criminal. Furthermore, she knows I love her unconditionally, independent of her actions.

Elaine recalled that her mother would call her a brat (and even a snot-nosed brat) as a child. She relates, "My mother would spend time in arguments convincing me that I had dark motives of manipulation and selfishness. As a young child, I would spend hours, days, and years wondering if I really did have evil motives. In my heart, I think I knew I didn't, but I figured there must be some truth to what she said. There were too many times she pointed out and emphasized the worst in me, and it has impacted my self-confidence dramatically. As an adult, I've realized that I didn't deserve that, and that it's never okay to do that to children. I'm afraid that many people go through life believing they truly are a bad person and that early conditioning affects them throughout their life."

Hard things have to be said in any relationship, and loving words and actions make it bearable. If your loved ones know you don't visualize them as a villain, it makes it easier to change because they are simply ridding themselves of an undesirable trait, instead of feeling completely undesirable.

Power in Positivity

A few years ago, someone hit the side of our car. The perpetrator didn't leave a note and therefore did not pay for the damage. Sadly, we didn't have money to pay for the repair, so the car remained in its smashed state. Every time I got in the car and watched the rust stains spread, it made me feel mopey and embarrassed. At my request, my husband popped the dented metal out as much as he could. The thing is that it took him a year to do this ten minute job. I was certainly annoyed that such a simple task had taken so long, but I was not less grateful towards him because of the elapsed time. When he finally finished, he was my knight in shining armor. I really felt he was wonderful for fixing the door, and tried to show him my appreciation.

We should reinforce the positive, not by simply omitting the negative, but with sincere compliments or gratitude. I could have stayed silent, refusing to acknowledge my husband's efforts, or complained and told him he was a bum for not fixing the door months earlier, but that is not what I wanted him to remember or become. I wanted him to realize how happy it made me.

Had I laid into him about taking forever to do anything I asked and then complained when he finally did do it, what would be his motivation to do something for me again? He would think nothing is ever good enough for me and wonder why he should waste his time. In such a scenario, I would be falsely prophesying that he was lazy and that he would be falsely prophesying I was never content. Imagine how that might impact our relationship the next time something in our home, like our marriage, needed to be fixed?

In this situation, there was a positive outcome for both my husband and me, but there were many other times I didn't compliment my husband or children when I should have. There were too many days I said all the wrong things and eagerly watched like a hawk to pounce on any mistake. It is easy to remember or see the negative. Make it a point to pay attention to the good things and forgive your family for taking one year or ten years to finish the job.

We snickered as my good friend reenacted her fury at the oil spot on her driveway. After waiting months for her husband to change the oil, she had yelled from the front porch, "I can't believe you are changing the oil in the driveway. How dumb is that? You could have gone on the grass or backed up five more feet in the road, but no, you had to change it in the driveway, and now our driveway will never be the same again!" She now refers to this moment of exaggerated drama as the redneck oil change.

She admitted to me later that she would never have said those things to a friend or neighbor, and that she really was appreciative of his efforts. Her poor husband never knew of her unspoken gratitude. At times, we are more grateful, patient, and gracious with neighbors than our family. We expect our family to automatically know we appreciate what they do, but we can't resist pointing out the sticky pancake left on the table. We often become impatient with their annoying behaviors and harbor the fear that if we don't express our criticisms, then they are just going to repeat the horrifying act or maintain what we believe to be their false perceptions.

A friend of mine told me of a time when he was a teenager. As he was trudging through his daily labor in the kitchen, he washed under appliances, scrubbed what he deemed were the already sparkling crevices, and ultimately did his very best adolescent job. When he was done, his mom appraised his work and redid the job. What mother hasn't done this or at least been seriously tempted to react this way? We often gravitate towards the negative. Sometimes our tunnel vision allows us only to see what is wrong, rather than that which has been done well, which makes it easy to be dissatisfied by the efforts of our family members.

When this young man had finished, the kitchen looked excellent to him, and he was feeling rather proud and even macho about his efforts. He had spent a long time trying to do well on a job he wasn't thrilled about to start with, but persevered and tried to impress his mom. His esteem crumpled as he watched his mother exhibit her dissatisfaction. He was no longer proud of his efforts and lost the motivation he had once had to do a pleasing job in the future. He now knew his mom was going to redo whatever he did. He freely admits from that point on, when it came to housework, he put forth a dismal effort.

As this young man's experience teaches us, self-personification and self-fulfilling prophecy manifest themselves not just in verbal form, but in our actions as well. His mom didn't tell him he did a bad job, but her actions spoke clearly: his best was not good enough. She never intended to hurt his feelings or make him feel his work was not good enough, but that is the clear message she sent. Maybe, instead of just doing it for him or telling him he did a bad job, it would be more effective for his mother to point out the parts that were done to her satisfaction. After all, who doesn't like being complimented? If correction was still needed, she could have asked him to redo those areas or she could have helped him.

Often, I justify correction on the premise of being practical, but who am I kidding? Clean kitchens aren't a necessity for happiness, and family life is rarely practical. My friend later said, "It seems the goal was not how to raise the child or help his self-esteem, but to have a clean kitchen. The goal was askew and overlooked the priority of parenthood. It is hard to change our self-made goals such as, 'the kitchen must be clean in order for me to be happy,' and realize that cleanliness might not be happiness but happiness is cleanliness."

We need to personify positive qualities and attitudes that will in turn help those around us to do the same. We can only do this if we are looking for the positive things, not just the practical and perfect.

Listen to the Chatter

While working on a task, the dialogue I hear flutters in and out between my own organized thoughts. I'm trying to listen, but I can't seem to focus on the words; they are coming so fast. They sound so familiar. I finally pull myself out of my own thoughts and I realize the words are my daughter's. She's been telling me a story and is now asking me a question about it. In my guilt, I pitifully admit I wasn't listening well and could she please repeat.

"Don't you like my stories mom? I really hate it when you don't listen to me." Feeling like the world's worst mom,

I tell her I really do want to hear what she has to say. I have compassion on her as I am reminded of the maddening moments when I try to talk to my husband while he is on the computer or watching TV, and how my husband might feel when I'm talking to my sister on the phone and he wants to tell me about his day.

The situation is simple. My daughter has something to say to me. In her mind, it is important, and it hurts her feelings when I tune her out. If I tell her I am really interested, my lack of attention communicates to her that the opposite is true. By not listening to my daughter, I am telling her that her thoughts and ideas are not worth listening to. Imagine how she may personify that. Sending the message that her ideas aren't worth listening to could easily lead her to believe they really aren't any good. Her confidence could plummet, and she could soon believe that if her thoughts and ideas are unimportant, then she is unimportant. If we don't listen to our family, they will find someone that will. That someone might be a trusted friend, the secretary at work, or the teenager doing drugs on the corner. My daughter is only nine years old; imagine her life in eight more years if I continue to ignore her when she tells me things she deems important. I want my family to come to me. I want to hear about their lives and help them succeed. I want to listen.

My sister Heather had an epiphany one day as her son persisted in repetitively voicing a concern she felt she had already addressed. She was fast becoming irritated at his inability and unwillingness to listen to her because she already knew what he was going to say, she knew she was right, and she wanted to move on. He was feeling unsatisfied because he needed to be heard and felt like she didn't care. Her hypocrisy suddenly shattered her stubbornness as she realized that she kept telling her son to listen to her when she would not listen to him. With this new realization, she closed her mouth and listened to everything he had to say. He then listened as she explained her feelings about the issue at hand. Almost as quickly as the argument began, it came to a close. Even though in the end her son still needed correction, he felt loved and validated because his mom listened to him. She said of the instance, "If you don't listen to them they fight and fight until you do. They don't necessarily want to be right, they just want to be heard."

Let your family know they are worth listening to, and give them the time it takes to listen to them, discuss with them, and give feedback to them. In my college days, I took a class that had a section on listening techniques. Eagerly wanting to share my newly acquired skills, I rushed home, and in the middle of a sentence in which my roommate was telling me something, I blurted out, "Do you want to learn good listening skills?" We had a lot of good laughs about it, and I have thought about it many times since. How often do we find ourselves in this situation? We want our families to listen to us, but are we listening to them?

Listening can be the catalyst that brings peace into our lives. Driving home from the store on an exceptionally hot, miserable, and tiring afternoon, my daughter began reciting items on a few receipts she had found at the store. She was excited and felt it necessary to read off all three receipts word for word. My son was trying to tell me a story. My two-year-old was screaming, "Mom!" and pointing at something awe inspiring every thirty seconds. The neighbor kid tagging along was singing passionately to the music on the radio, and my four-year-old was crying because we bought macaroni and cheese instead of pizza. I wanted to turn up the music and tune down the 'crazy' flying around me, but I mustered my patience and walked into the now raging storm.

I acknowledged the two-year-old with "Wows" and "Isn't that neat?" I made a comment about my son's story, told my four-year-old we would get pizza for her birthday and expressed it was my opinion that my oldest daughter didn't really need to read me someone else's receipt. To this response, she replied that she thought it was neat and really wanted to read it to me. So, I listened and slowly the tsunami around me began to dissipate. Sometimes, all a family needs in order to put out a fire, clear up a miscommunication, or feel and believe they are loved, is one person who is willing to listen.

The Need to Compete

Sometimes we get caught up in our own craziness and find ourselves thinking or acting like whatever we are doing is more important, more difficult, or more life-altering than what our spouse or children are doing or experiencing. When this happens we are not listening, caring, supporting, or helping our family members. We may simply be solidifying their long-held and self-made personification that they don't matter.

Picture this story from my animated life. The events of this day really did happen but my husband's response, which is usually very thoughtful and loving, has been exaggerated for examples sake. In my fatigue, I feebly cried to my husband that I was perturbed with the kids for using all the clean blankets and towels to make a fort outside in the dirt.

During their outside adventure, the baby flooded the bathroom and hallway. I had to use muddy blankets to clean up the water because the kids used all the towels outside. While I was doing so, the two-year-old started throwing eggs around the kitchen, and dinner burned because I was cleaning up the eggs. Without blinking an eye, my husband tells me how much worse his day was than mine, blowing into oblivion my deeply rooted insanity, almost as if what I said never existed. I didn't tell my husband how tired I was so he could tell me he was more tired.

To this, I found myself thinking, "No one listens and no one cares. I'm not even going to bother." When a person constantly feels outdone and their family shows little regard for their efforts or sacrifice, it can be a manifestation to them that they are not worth it and neither are their efforts. Suddenly, you have a breeding ground for low motivation and invalidated people who no longer believe their efforts are worthwhile.

Listening without comparing and competing is important. It allows your loved ones to feel needed and appreciated. It helps them get over a bump or bad day. It validates them in their goals and desires and motivates them to keep trying even when it's hard. Next time you're tempted to compete in the 'life's worst moments' contest, don't. Just listen. There is nothing wrong with having a bad day and sharing it, but try to listen and support rather than outdo. Wait for a more appropriate or thoughtful moment to share your experience and share it in a way that doesn't belittle your family members' experiences. Practice good listening techniques, make eye contact, give a hug, and use verbal cues. Show them they are worth your time and that what they do is important and worthy of their best efforts.

One evening after I complimented my son about what a great job he did sweeping the floor, my daughter immediately chimed in, "Didn't I do a good job?" To which I responded, "Yes, but remember, just because he did a good job doesn't mean you did a bad job." Family life is not a competition. Just because your spouse or children are good at something or succeed in a way that you haven't doesn't mean you can't be happy. When my husband started his business, I was happy for him but sad for me. I was sad because he was fulfilling his big dream while mine was on hold. After feeling sorry for myself, I realized that just because great things were happening for him, it in no way meant I was a failure. It was his moment, and I could be happy about that without any jealousy or need to down play his success.

People Rise to the Occasion

When given the opportunity, people will rise to the occasion. They will do things you, others, or even themselves didn't think they would or could do. To do this, they must be given the opportunity to succeed. For children, this may require us to avoid fretting about the chocolaty mess gushing over our kitchen counters or the misuse of supplies and tools as our children create their own recipe for chocolate cake. This might mean we encourage our spouse, even if we don't love their ideas or if we are nervous about the outcomes of their endeavors. Everyone needs someone who believes in them and who will be their biggest fan and supporter. This is something that often requires a great deal of trust and patience. It is hard to hand over the car keys to the inexperienced and likely distracted teenager or help your spouse prepare for the interview that will send you packing across the country.

Every time my husband is behind the wheel and I thwart a car accident by utilizing my perfected backseat driving skills, I ask him, "How do you survive without me?" He, of course, reminds me that we rarely drive together and he has never caused a wreck. I am forced to silently admit that he really does survive without me telling him to drive slower or stop quicker.

Sometimes trusting and helping our loved ones succeed and rise to the occasion means that we must take action to prepare them and then give up some control and begin to trust in their abilities. I am always teasing my children that they need to stop growing up because I will miss them too much. It is exciting for me to watch them learn new things and see their personalities and talents develop, but there is always a part of me that wants to safely hide them in bubble wrap to preserve the sweetness of their childhood. This security can be appealing, but in reality it is both impossible and absurd. I ache inside when my children make poor choices, get made fun of, or fail. But if I don't let them go, and support them along the way, they will never rise to the occasion of life.

I have realized my children's lives are a constant repeat of that first day I dropped them off to kindergarten. It was exciting and scary for both of us. For the first time, I had to undo the bubble wrap because if I let it remain, it would inhibit their growth. With a tear rolling down my cheek, I hoped that both my and their preparation would be enough to succeed, enough to help them fit in, and enough for them to be happy. Hopefully, the love and care we present to our families will prepare them to succeed individually and as a whole.

My daughter desperately wanted to learn her times tables. Her school class had not yet begun to teach multiplication. I was tempted to tell her to wait for her class and stick with addition and subtraction, but I knew she would be disappointed. I also knew she could do it and that she would love it, but I wasn't ready for her to be that smart yet. My daughter was very capable of learning multiplication, she just needed me to unwrap the protective layering. She needed someone to show her and supply her with a multiplication chart and a little motivation. I told her she could have my art set if she could pass of her times tables through the number twelve. She is now becoming very sufficient in multiplication and can do it just fine without me. In order to succeed, our families need this same support, trust, and freedom. We shouldn't limit them only to life's addition and subtraction.

My husband drives to work every day without me, but even when he comes home with a speeding ticket, I don't tell him I'm taking him to work tomorrow. I tell him to go back to work and make enough money to pay for the ticket. When our spouse or children make mistakes we don't tell them to quit, that they are losers, or that "we told them so." Like us, they will make mistakes and they don't need to hear how stupid they are because they likely have plenty of insecurities about that already. What they need to hear is encouragement: "You can do this," "Don't give up," and "I'll help you."

Show your family you have confidence in them. Everyone has hidden skills, talents, and desires, and in a family, we should support and help our loved ones have the confidence they need to succeed. It will take patience, time, trust and forgiveness, but it will make a difference. Allow your family to rise to the occasion. They will likely surprise you and themselves.

Defend Your Family

Defending the ones you love is vital. I often hear others complain about their children or spouse to friends, family, or co-workers. I am openly guilty of this as well. Our hurtful words are rarely meant to hurt, but they do. By stating what we perceive to be reality, we may think that we are simply letting go of frustration, but even gossiping about reality is hurtful. When a friend says something negative about you, it hurts. If a stranger says something negative to you, it hurts. So imagine how much more it would hurt when someone you love and who should love you verbalizes negativity about you to others. You might begin to believe what they say is true, become hurt that they betrayed your trust, and call into question their love for you. In these situations, remember the golden rule. If you don't want your family members to say negative things about you, then you best not say negative things about them.

My aunt always used to remind me, "Children have big ears and they hear everything." Be careful what you say and be thoughtful of how you say it. If you complain that your spouse is never home, never gets anything done, only plays video games, or is a fun hater, not only will others believe it, but you, your spouse, and your children will eventually internalize it and begin to believe it too.

Think of your anxiety and discontent with your family as a smoldering fire. You have two options: You can fuel the fire or smother it. When you are denigrating to others about your family, your smoldering fire expands with the fuel you gave it. Feelings and thoughts spawned in the heat of frustration can fuel the flames into a bonfire. You may even begin to focus so much on the negative that those glaring faults may become all you are able to see in your loved ones. Without meaning to, you have degraded the person or people you should love the most.

We should be protecting our family instead of exposing their weaknesses, intimacies, or secrets. Sheri said, "My family is a family of gossipers. My mother is the head gossip and she has taught her children well. When I was about eleven years old, I had a crush on a boy (not unusual), but I was a little shy about it. I was actually very shy at the time and didn't talk about how I felt to anyone. I decided to tell my mom, assuming that she was the one person I could trust. A couple of weeks later, I was with my dad and he asked me about the boy that I liked, and I knew my mother had breached my trust. Now as a parent, I see that this may not have seemed like a breach of my trust, but at the time it did. I felt betrayed. After that experience, I did not confide in my mother. As I grew older, I saw that even though my evaluation at the time may not have been fair, it was accurate. I saw my mother share intimate experiences about herself, her children, or anyone else who had confided in her. It was always done without the approval of the person whose experience it was and in what I felt were inappropriate ways. Fortunately, I learned in my teenage years that my dad was the opposite. He became the parent I could talk to and confide in without judgment or the fear of having my thoughts and feelings exposed."

None of us want our secrets revealed, weaknesses exposed, or intimacies shared. As families we can create trust and offer security to our loved ones by avoiding gossip. Sometimes, it is helpful to talk with a friend about worries or concerns to release anger without releasing it on your family, or to discover you are not the only one who has an imperfect husband, wife or children. However, we must be cautious with such attempts. My sister-in-law put it perfectly: "Problems that need to be resolved should be resolved with the person in question, not with others who aren't involved." Tender emotions shared in trust should be kept in trust.

Use positive self-personification as a way to magnify your use of the Red Punch Experiment—showing love to the ones you love the most. I would be so much happier to come home to a husband who openly praises me to friends and co-workers, rather than complaining about me or putting me down. Make an effort to personify positivity, and when you are uncertain about a situation, err on the side of trust. Give the benefit of the doubt. Listen to your family, even when you feel they are not listening to you. Be thoughtful of your family's experiences and feelings. Your problems and joys are just as important as theirs. Don't try to outdo their problems or joys, or feel like you are not good enough because they succeeded. Remember to do unto others as you would have them do unto you. Allow your family the environment, support, and opportunities they need to succeed. Make an effort to defend your loved ones rather than attack them, complain about them, or put them down.

When you communicate with your family, ask yourself if you are helping them personify themselves in an encouraging light. Are you helping them fulfill and create positive images of themselves or negative images? The way we view and treat our loved ones truly affects the happiness in our lives and in our homes and has momentary as well as lasting effects. Viewing your family in a positive light won't solve all your problems, but it will foster a safer home environment and instill positivity in those you love.

CHAPTER SEVEN

Peace is Persuasive: Resolving Conflict

Challenge: Choose to forgive an injustice you have been harboring

As teardrops began to well up inside Ella's eyes, I started to wonder if having a clean house was worth it. She was upset because the mop kept breaking, and I told her she was going to have to finish the kitchen floor on her hands and knees, with a rag. Julia had been on time-out for an hour, screaming about how she would never pick up the hallway. I set Jackson on the bed so I could vacuum, but when I turned around he had tumbled to the floor and was making a raging flood of crocodile tears. I had picked him up to console him when Ella began sobbing. Daniel had punched her in the stomach because she yelled at him when he tried to walk across her newly cleaned and still wet floor. "This isn't worth it," I told myself as the bitterness set in that my husband was working weekends again. I held the baby, told the other kids what I expected, and walked away until I could achieve a sense of humanity.

Every family has explosions and I don't know of a single family that enjoys them. These are obviously not the moments we live for; these are the moments we want to minimize and eliminate. In my moment of frustration, I kept thinking, "What do I do? There has to be a solution to this that I can feel good about." Not until I calmed down could I see this wasn't as big a deal as we were all making it.

In need of peaceful resolution, I nixed the room cleaning and any other jobs we had not yet begun. Daniel and I had a chat that involved things like, "You don't have a right to hit other people," "How would you feel if you were mopping the floor and everyone kept walking on it making it dirty again?" and "Does being mean make you feel good inside?" I decided Daniel should finish mopping the floor for Ella so he could understand what it was like and so he could help her feel better. Julia finally got tired of being in time-out and took the dreaded two minutes to pick up the floor. Jackson ran off to play, and Ella decided to show Daniel where she had already mopped so he wouldn't have to do it twice.

We were all so caught up in the moment we couldn't see past our own frustrations. As I began to regain some perspective, I learned some fascinating things about our adventure.

1. Conflict will always arise. You can't put even similar personalities under the same roof for several years and expect everything to be perfect all the time. A.P. Herbert said, "The concept of two people living together for twenty-five years without a serious dispute

suggests a lack of spirit only to be admired in sheep"
(Sherrin, 2008).

2. We often blow things out of proportion, as we saw with Julia, who cried for an hour over two minutes of work.

3. Some battles are not worth it, like making the kids clean their room at a particularly frustrating time. Sometimes, we need to step back from the situation and decide whether the battle is worth the fight. Deciding which battles are worth it depends on what's important to you.

4. Unexpected things happen, like Jackson's fall off the bed.

5. There is usually an underlying cause to the contention. Part of the reason my kids were getting upset was because they had made other plans and had hoped to do other things.

6. Discipline is important, and how we discipline makes a difference, as we saw with Daniel when he had to mop the floor for Ella.

7. Blame is often a swift but ineffective response to conflict. We all blamed something or someone for our problems. Ella blamed me because I told her she had to mop by hand. Daniel claimed it was Ella's fault he hit her, and I convinced myself that it was Bryce's fault all this happened because he wasn't home to assist.

8. Selfishness is in every conflict, as was manifested in all of our actions. I was pushing my desires on the

kids; they didn't want to help because they would rather do other things.

9. How we treat each other has everything to do with our ability to solve the conflict and restore peace. When Ella treated Daniel with kindness and I administered discipline with love, Daniel did the required job instead of retreating.

10. I noticed forgiveness and service were our resolutions, as when Ella forgave Daniel for punching her and then decided to help him. Forgiveness was the only thing that made it so we could move on.

Just because we have moments that are not perfect doesn't mean our happily *ever after* isn't knocking at the door, waiting for an invitation. As my children and I began to be more thoughtful of one another, our tone of voice changed. Our anger diminished as we listened to each other's needs and our compassion and patience increased as we began to help each other. It took us a little while, but we simply had to be wise enough to let peace in and let selfishness out.

What Are We Arguing About?

One evening, my children and I were preparing to have guests over. Like the Red Punch Experiment suggests, I was in a fluster trying to make the house perfect. My husband wasn't home to help prepare for the very guests *he* had invited. In fact he had been gone for most of the week due to work and would arrive home just in time to find dinner lavishly spread, the house scoured, and the children tidy, or at least without dirt and food smeared on their chins. I had been trying really hard to be loving, patient, and kind with my children, but their persistent defiance overwhelmed my already overburdened self.

I was head to head with one of my kids at a stubborn impasse as I tried to compel her to clean out the dishwasher. Her continued refusal to do this simple job pushed me to tears. She immediately felt remorse for my pain, of which she naively felt she was the cause. I felt so bad when she also started crying because I knew my tears were not because of her, but from deeper issues. I was tired, stressed, and overwhelmed because my husband had been out of town for so long. From this experience, I learned that the causes for most of our conflicts run deeper than whatever it is we are arguing about. If the cause of our conflicts runs deeper than the perceived argument, it would make sense that the solution is deeper than mere discipline or the desire for changed behavior. The solution will be found in love, not force or animosity. It's not only the discipline you give or the change you expect, but the love that goes into that discipline or change.

Experience has shown me that conflict usually inspires more conflict and love usually inspires more love. When someone attacks you, is angry with you, or expects change in you that you don't desire, the first and most natural response is defensiveness. We build trenches and arm our fortress with the most profound and scarring weapons. We bring blame, sarcasm, and venom. We put up walls so that no thoughtless word can penetrate us, and then we begin our counterattack.

When we attempt to resolve conflict, it is important to remember the desired end product. It seems obvious that our desire should be to resolve the conflict, but sometimes we get caught up in an obsessive need to be right using whatever means necessary to win, which only intensifies the very conflict we wish to resolve (Arbinger, 2006).

While driving home one evening, my husband and I listened to the radio station, where a couple that had just celebrated their fiftieth wedding anniversary was being interviewed. The host of the show was amazed they could be married so long and asked them how they did it. The husband quickly replied, "We learned the phrase early on: 'you might be right.'" I logged that away, and the next time my husband and I were having an argument that I began to yawn at, I finally said, "Bryce, you might be right." My husband took it to heart and was confident he had won the argument. Feeling secure in his triumph, he replied with a brief, "Thanks."

"What a lame-o," I thought. "How could he really believe I thought he was right?" With a tinge of arsenic, I replied, "Did you hear what I said? You *might* be right?" I should have kept my mouth shut, but I couldn't. I had to tear away his victory and shrivel his satisfaction. He really could have been right, but I couldn't let him be. I couldn't let the issue be resolved because his cockiness annoyed me and threatened my pride.

The point in resolving conflict is not to be the winner. It is not to have the last word or to triumph with the most heartless attack. The point and desire of any conflict should be to solve the problem. Our hardened and cold armor doesn't really solve our problem and neither does our harsh attacks. We are human and therefore feel the pain of a cutting remark. As the Arbinger Institute suggests, we take our pain and are inspired to continue our assault until the cycle of attack finally ends with empty victories, wounded hearts, and higher walls (Arbinger, 2006). The good news is that we can break this cycle with love. If we are going to resolve conflict, we need to start at the root of the problem and be humble enough and wise enough to set aside harsh remarks, pride, and selfishness.

Selfishness Cannot Bring Happiness or Resolution

Selfishness cannot bring happiness. Why do we get angry and say mean things to the people who love us the most? Why do we often struggle to resolve conflict? Selfishness! It is easiest to identify selfishness by being aware of statements that begin with *I*. *I* am tired of doing the dishes by myself, *I* worked so hard today, *I* don't want to clean my room, *I* want to go to my friend's house, or *I* need a break. In a family, it is difficult to find true happiness until the people around us are also happy. If we focused more on each other rather than ourselves, we would find most of our needs would be met and many of our conflicts would dissolve.

We know the ins and outs, joys and sorrows, and fears and frustrations of the ones we love, and if we choose, we can create deep festering wounds through selfishness. A lifetime of heartache and contention are perpetuated when we, as loved ones, take advantage of the inner workings of the heart for our own selfish designs. I could have belittled my kids that dreadful morning we spent cleaning the house and picked at their insecurities to guilt them into doing what I wanted, but to what end? It would have been only to fulfill my selfish desires. Families work on a system of trust. Don't betray that trust to gain an advantage, no matter how right you think you are.

Make yourself approachable—someone your family can trust their emotions with. A simple apology can heal so many wounds. Maybe the problems you face in your relationship can't be resolved your way. So much about enjoying our families, resolving conflict, and finding happiness has to do with letting go of our own pride and remembering how wonderful and important these people really are.

One of the most repeated and heated arguments of our marriage, as you may have already guessed, has been the battle over time. To be specific, I have felt like my husband doesn't spend enough time with the family, and he has felt cornered with his desire to provide his family with the necessities and comforts of life. The argument recently resurfaced. I told him it had been too long since he had taken me on a date and I was expecting a night out. He maintained that his business would only be super busy for a short while, and that we would have time to go out after the business rush. This of course did not appease me, as this is not even close to the first time we have had this conversation, and I knew he would always be busy. I was feeling sure of my argument, just as he was of his and neither of us would budge. I wanted alone time with my husband and he was feeling that he needed to do his job and that taking a day off would cost him dearly. I felt like he didn't care about me and he felt I was being unfair.

As we both continued to press our point, we were getting angry and resolving nothing. We took a bit of time to think away from the heat of the situation. I didn't feel like my desires were selfish; rather, I felt they were important, but as I pondered my husband's predicament, I realized his desires weren't selfish either. They were real concerns, as he would lose five hundred dollars for every day he didn't meet his deadline. I knew he felt stuck and I made a resolve to love him even if he felt he couldn't take time for me or family. I also decided I would try to help him with his jobs in any way I could. Unbeknownst to me, my husband had realized that I, too, was struggling, and that it was important for him to take time with the family because he had always been so busy. He decided to enact a company policy that would allow him and his employees to have two nights a week that were guaranteed to be open, despite the inconvenience or loss it would be to the company.

We were in a hard situation. Though in the beginning we were not being selfish in our desires, we were being selfish with our unwillingness to see and understand the other's concerns, or to budge on the stance we had taken. Instead of resolving our concerns, we were making them worse. What is more, we could see no solution to our problem that would not require sacrifice or loss on one or the other's part. Both of our needs were legitimate and in order to work for the best solution possible, we had to put aside our selfishness and remind ourselves how much we cared about each other. It took great humility and love for my husband to do what he did and it made me feel important. His actions were solely motivated by his love for his children and me. I have no doubt similar arguments will arise again, but I know if my husband and I can put aside our selfishness and remember our love for one another, we will be able to resolve any problem.

Even the most difficult problems in our relationships can be solved if we can let go of selfishness. Many of our conflicts will have to be resolved with sacrifice as ours did. Sometimes we have to give up things that are important to us in order to solve our issues. What a wonderful opportunity our conflict provided to both my husband and me to show love to the one we love most.

Familiarity Helps Resolve Conflict

The way with which we handle conflict has a lot to do with our personalities. Some personalities are very intense and controlling, while others are more likely to bend to the will of another. Some personality types are loud, boisterous, and pushy when resolving conflict. Some are quiet and timid, while others let the conflict roll off their back like it doesn't even exist. When we are resolving conflict, we need to examine the personality of both ourselves and those who we are experiencing conflict with. We should not treat people like they don't have a clue or like they are always wrong and we are always right. On the other hand, sometimes no matter how much we dislike confrontation, we have to have the courage to engage and to share our feelings in order to healthily resolve conflict. The silent stew is just as counter-productive as the thunderous boom.

Everyone wants his or her opinions and beliefs to be respected and valued. In order for real conflict resolution to take place, people need to feel safe. Being considerate and respectful of your loved ones' personalities and ability to handle confrontation allows for open communication. It helps to avoid construction of defensive walls which are often needed to deflect the harmful words the other is desperately hurling. If you can remove the walls of defense through love, communication can flow. Instead of spending your time coming up with counterattacks, you will be able to listen to the real underlying issues. Don't be the kind of person who walks all over the people you love and don't be the kind of person who gets walked all over.

Knowing my husband and children's personalities helps me to know how to confront difficult situations with them and it helps me know when I need to back off. I learned that when working with my husband, his intensity, which is one of the things I love about him, often overwhelms me. When I feel this way, I sometimes need a break, after which I can return to an important discussion with him and leave my pending aneurysm checked at the door.

The same is true with my children. I know which ones need a little push and which ones will walk the other way if they are pressed or feel attacked. My husband's aunt Keri put it perfectly when she told me, "I finally figured it out. I am Mr. Rabbit and my son is Tigger. When I instill order, he bounces right out of the walls I have created for him." This realization, though based on fictional characters, made all the difference. It helped her understand how they could come together in love and compromise and have happier, better conflict resolution.

We need to take the time to understand the members of our family. Discover differences, but be careful not to use each other's weaknesses to attack or promote our own agenda. Ella and Bryce are Mr. Rabbit. They enjoy order and control. They are good leaders and need to be appreciated. Daniel is a Pooh Bear. He is sweet and innocent, desiring to simply take care of what needs to be done, while somehow always landing himself in trouble. Julia is a Piglet. She is happy and in need of lots of love and protection. Jackson is a Tigger, who loves fun and does not appreciate boundaries. I am Christopher Robin. I appreciate security. I am a mild mannered problem solver, and I want everyone to be happy.

Maybe we are a Tigger or a Pooh Bear. Maybe our spouse or child is an Eeyore or a Mr. Rabbit. No matter who our loved ones personify, they are all important characters with vital talents and skills. The Hundred Acre Wood wouldn't be the same without each lovable character, nor would the Packard family be the same without each wonderful person present. We don't always get along, nor do we do things the same way, but we are all needed.

Blame is Poison

When conflicts arise, blame is often our go-to defense. When my kids and I were cleaning and our emotions were heightened, everyone believed that his or her frustrations and problems arose because of someone else. We were all so quick to blame, but until we took responsibility, healing could not occur. Blame destroys trust, love, peace, and happiness. We often don't want to admit that our problems are our own fault and so, by default, we toss responsibility on our family, spouse, children, or parents. Maybe they really do play a role in whatever tragedy has found its way through our doors, but blaming never improves the situation. Regardless of what situations have been created by those around us, our reaction is our own and we cannot blame that on anyone.

Blame is toxic; it spreads from one source to another until it becomes an epidemic. My husband and I happened to be visiting a family while they were doing some home improvement projects. They struggled immensely to complete the task without casting blame on the other person. They kept bringing up situations that happened years before to prove that their current situation was the other's fault. One person would make a cutting and blaming remark and, in defense, the other would retaliate with a similar remark. I observed to myself that the things they kept blaming each other for had little to do with the task at hand, but once the blame started, it was hard to stop.

When trying to resolve conflict, we shouldn't waste our time with blame or try to justify its use. Even when someone makes a mistake, especially a big mistake, the last thing they want to hear is blame. Blame will not solve any problems.

One hectic day, I dropped my two oldest kids at a friend's house and headed to the store. The car was so quiet, and in my rush, I left my youngest in the car while I went into the grocery store. I didn't even realize it until I was on my way out. I panicked, dropped all my things, and ran to the car in terror. I was so scared I thought I was going to vomit. I was lucky; fortunately, it was a cold day and my child was safe and sitting contently in her car seat.

In my eyes, this was the worst parenting moment of my life. In fact, I never talk about it because it makes me feel so awful. With tears in my eyes and a shaky voice, I admitted to my husband what I had done. Imagine the love and care I felt when he put his arms around me and said, "It's okay. She's okay." He didn't say, "How could you be in such a hurry that you forgot our child? How irresponsible! She could have died!" He didn't need to say these things. I already knew them and was truly traumatized by it. Because of his love and compassion in place of blame, I loved him all the more. I knew, and still know, that I could trust him with anything. He won't blame me or attack me, but will instead show love and compassion, working for a solution if needed.

Keep in mind when conflict arises that you are looking for a solution, not a battle. Even with the most difficult choices, problems, and mistakes, if you remove blame from the situation, they will be solved quicker, less hurtfully, more peacefully, and with much more love.

Kids Have Feelings Too

Sometimes I think we forget our children are humans who can act. Instead, we treat them like beings to be acted upon. They are often perceived as a hindrance to our *ever after*. We tell them to do things we don't want to do, we tell them how they feel is wrong, or we tell them the bump on their head isn't really as painful as they think. As my own family tried to resolve conflict over cleaning the house, it was important for me to realize my children had ideas of how the day should go and had things they would rather be doing. Understanding that gave me more compassion for them as I tried to mediate the chaos and conflict.

When conflict must be resolved with our children, how we envision them makes all the difference. Don't forget to use the Red Punch Experiment here. If we are not intentional in treating our children with respect and love, resolving conflict with our children can lead to a lot of baggage down the road for both parent and child. Jodi, my sister-in-law, expressed that, "Children are not property. They grow up to be adults and will remember how you have treated them." I often hear parents apologize to their adult children for how they treated them and resolved conflict with them. I'm guessing we all have and will have moments in which apologies to our children are appropriate and necessary, but such experiences with our children can be minimized greatly by treating our children respectfully.

As I grew up, my feelings, beliefs, and desires did not always align with those of my parents. When a disagreement about something would arise, I knew I could talk to my parents about my feelings and desires. They always considered my point of view and how I felt about it. Sometimes they would turn in my favor and sometimes they held their ground. When I broke our family rules, my parents maintained the same respect while administering discipline. They did not mistreat me or use cruelty. They listened to me, respected me, and taught me while still protecting me from my youthful lack of wisdom.

Resolving conflict with our children can be a never ending task, but if we can remember that we love them and respect them as individuals, it will be easier to show that love to them in difficult circumstances. Our children, old and young, have great emotion and retain the words and actions they hear and see. They feel pain, have valid thoughts and ideas, and deserve our respect and our love.

True Change Comes from Within

In an exasperating moment with our son, we were at a loss as to how we should discipline him. He had done some very hurtful and disrespectful things, and the only thing we hadn't tried was spanking him. Neither my husband nor I wanted to spank him. We didn't feel like it would help, but we also did not think what he had done could go without consequence. In our desperation to teach him, we decided to let him be Mom for a week. It sounded like a great idea with fabulous teaching opportunities.

First, we wanted him to realize that his jobs in the family were not as hard as he imagined, and second, that he needed to manage his time better and be more respectful of the people around him. We implemented the discipline immediately and our child was so excited because obviously there is no greater opportunity in life than to be Mom. We wrote out an hour-by-hour schedule for him to follow. We told him he could ask for help, but that he was in charge of making sure everything got done. He was in charge of choosing TV time, play time, and chore time. We told him if meals were not prepared on time that we would feed the little kids but not him. We informed him that he had until 8:30 p.m. to complete his daily jobs with help from others. If he did not complete the jobs by this time, he would have to complete them on his own, as it would be bedtime for everyone else.

Our child thrived the first day. He loved it. We had to remind him of a lot of things, but he did it and reveled in his newfound role. By Tuesday, the excitement was wearing off rapidly, and by Wednesday he had an absolute meltdown. Meals were not made, dishes were left undone, and the house was in a massive state of disorder. Feeling frustrated myself, I was about to take away the trip to the water park that he and his sister had earned by reading five hundred minutes in a single month. It was a school program to encourage children to read. Luckily, before I made this unpardonable mistake, I thought twice. He had already earned this trip. It was a reward for something he already did and taking it away would be wrong.

So, with the house in shambles and dinner left undone, we went to the water park. We bought pizza for the kids but our son did not get to share in it, because he had failed to make dinner. He made dinner when we arrived home, and we stuck with the original consequence. He had to do everything by himself because it was past 8:30 p.m. He was tired and frustrated but managed to finish the jobs. Needless to say, it was uphill from there. The morning after his discipline ended, he woke up with a huge smile on his face and said, "Good morning, real Mom." It made me laugh, because he wasn't the only one who was happy about this discipline ending.

We could have taken away our son's hard-earned trip to the water park, but what would our child have learned? Perhaps we would have taught that it is not worth working hard for things because they just get taken away in the end. Or perhaps we would have taught him that his parents do not keep their promises. Our son had already earned this trip by meeting the requirement the school had set, and we told him if he met the schools requirements to earn the ticket to the water park, we would take him. I want my son to trust me. I am grateful we had set up consequences and rules for his discipline before the water park incident so that I didn't get caught up in the heat of moment and break my promise.

Often, taking time to be a good parent and resolving conflict internally rather than forcing externally is the more time-consuming route. We could have spanked him and been done with the discipline in five minutes. Spanking our child would have externally stopped his actions for a moment, but there would have been no lasting effect. We also could have ignored the inappropriate behavior and moved on. Sometimes, having no consequence at all can be just as detrimental down the road as having too severe of a consequence. It can foster irresponsible behavior because it would teach that our actions do not have consequences. Discipline is an opportunity to teach correct principles and foster change.

It has been some time since this discipline, but its outcomes have been lasting. Every time our son does a job quickly and without complaint, I am so grateful we took the effort and the pains to foster internal change by providing him with experience, knowledge, and gratitude for those in his life that care about him.

Healthy discipline is a path to greater freedom for your children, especially your teenagers. It is a tool to teach the importance of trust, power, responsibility, and cooperation. It utilizes creativity and natural consequences, rather than physical force and manipulation. It instills sorrow and guilt rather than shame or embarrassment. Sorrow and guilt don't shame a child or destroy confidence, but rather teaches that they made a mistake and need to make recompense for it and learn from it.

Shame and manipulation, however, are hazardous. My mother in law said, "Manipulation perverts a child's outlook because it is not truth, and when we teach these false principles to our children through manipulation, it damages and abuses their self-esteem." Manipulation can coerce people into giving in to others selfish desires, but its motives and principles are askew. For example, my daughter Julia tried to manipulate me by telling me that if I didn't give her a fruit snack, I wouldn't be her mom. This is a lie. I will be her mom, no matter what. Even if I wasn't her mom, using this manipulation was a threat, intended to hurt my feelings so she could attain her desired outcome, which was getting a fruit snack. Manipulation often leads to shame.

Using shame frequently makes children feel that not only what they did is bad, but that they are a bad person for doing it. It may motivate them to stop what they are doing, but it will likely have a long lasting, negative impact on their life. Manipulation and shame teach a false sense of self and ideals. They are based on the assumption that people have bad motives and characteristics and that they cannot or will not change. We shouldn't force our children to do what we want using shame and manipulation. Instead, we should guide them by teaching boundaries and principles through discipline, appropriate guilt, and love.

My good friend Diane thoughtfully shared an experience she had with discipline growing up. "One evening I went out for a walk and I just decided not to go home. I ran away. My parents, like any other concerned parents, were sick with worry. When I resurfaced, I was prepared for serious discipline. I was waiting for my parents to take away my driver's license, yell at me, or ground me for life, but they didn't. My dad put me in the car and took me on a road trip so he could figure out what was going on and what had pushed me to run away. My parents most important concern was not 'how do we deal with her,' but rather 'what is wrong' and what could they do to fix it. When the reasons for my disappearance were discovered, it was only then that discipline was administered. My parents had waited to understand the situation before they decided what the best discipline was. You can be sure it was a long time before I was allowed to go on walks alone."

Diane's parents were intentional about their discipline. They took time to understand the situations surrounding her rebellious act because they wanted their daughter to know she was loved. They motivated change from within by helping their daughter feel safe with them. Their efforts taught her about life and helped her to trust them.

Diane said of this discipline, "I never felt like my parents were judging me, and because of that I knew they loved me and I knew that whatever I did, I could come to them for help or advice. Their concern for me made me think twice about the decisions I made. I learned so much about how to handle conflict and administer discipline with my own children. I learned that I needed to treat my children with respect whether they were right or wrong. I learned that I should never talk down to them, ridicule them, or roll my eyes at them. I learned that I needed to listen to their often misguided notions, and end each discipline and conversation with a hug and an 'I love you.' I also learned that it is my responsibility to teach my child. If I want a say in how my child turns out, I have to do my part."

We need to look down the road at the consequences that our discipline and actions could have on our children. We want our resolutions to instill trust, teach them, and provide our children with appropriate skills to manage conflict. Physical or manipulative force can cause fear and insecurities. It is hypocritical to tell your child you love them and care for them and that they are safe with you, while hurting them at the same time. It is difficult for a child to feel loved, cared for, and safe when they are being physically or emotionally harmed. What grounds have you given your children to trust you and respect you? Have you built a relationship with them in which they feel safe with you and understand your motives are based on your love for them rather than your impatience with them? When your teenage daughter has been sleeping around and has contracted a STD or gotten pregnant, will she feel safe coming to you? When your teenage son wrecks the car, is he going to be safe with you and your method of discipline? When your children have concerns, fears, or questions, are they going to feel secure coming to you for help and advice? Just as Diane's parents, we should discipline in a way that helps to build our relationships rather than break them down.

With all of this in mind, I cannot tell you the way you should discipline your children. Every child is different and responds to differing degrees and types of discipline. Be wise and intentional about what you do and say. I often gauge my level of discipline on my child. I start with the mildest discipline and increase according to my child's response and ability to learn from his or her mistakes. Most often, I find that natural consequences suffice. For example, if I tell my kid not to touch the burner because it's hot and they do it anyway, the natural consequence is that they get burned. But, if my child is trying to get into the oven, this is not an appropriate time for natural consequences and a more aggressive and prompt action would be needed. As you cross the line from the goal of internal change to mere external force, keep in mind that conflict resolution should be free from hypocrisy.

If you are married, be sure you and your spouse come to an agreement on what you feel is appropriate discipline for your children. My children often try to manipulate our system, and if we as parents are not on the same page, any discipline administered by my husband or me will be sabotaged by our own inconsistencies. Sometimes, I feel my husband is too aggressive in his discipline and sometimes, he feels I am too mild. When this happens, we try very hard to support each other in our choice and actions and voice our discontent with the other's methods, away from our children. We have been disciplining children for ten years, and because new situations with our children are always arising, we as a couple continually need to discuss, change, and improve our disciplining methods. My husband would add that we should beware of one-size-fits-all rules. When it comes to disciplining our children, it's imperative that we come to an agreement about how to discipline and what is okay in disciplining, and we both agree that we work together for the benefit of our children. When all is said and done, let love be your guide.

Fix the Leaks

Years ago, my father and mother were preparing for bed when my dad made a very innocent comment that triggered all of the pent up emotion and anger within my mother about previously unresolved conflicts in their marriage. This incident apparently became a very memorable ordeal. When I was getting married, they specifically brought up this story to teach me how important it is to resolve conflict when it arises. They told me to fix the leak so you wouldn't have a flood and to avoid wasted time in anger and hurt.

My grandmother reminded me that, for children, having immediate conflict resolution is best for two reasons. First, if you are anything like me, an hour after the incident you've forgotten all about it, and unless your child is eager to tell on themselves, nothing is resolved or learned. Second, children seem to learn more effectively immediately following whatever action took place because it is still fresh in their mind.

Often, we wait to resolve or discuss problems because we don't have time, are too upset, or don't enjoy confrontation. We allow tension to build and then explode later on at the slightest whim. It is appropriate to take some time to cool off, but resume resolution promptly, so you can move on with a feeling of peace.

When we wait to resolve conflict, it often leads to resentment. My children, husband, and I often visit my husband's parents in Colorado. I love visiting his parents and I feel it is worth the time and money we spend. However, I began resenting the fact that we would always spend our time and money visiting his parents and never mine. My children and husband had never visited my parent's home in Virginia. I understood that it was so much more expensive and time consuming to get to their home. However, I really wanted them to have experiences with my parents. My resentment was building quickly, and I knew I needed to discuss what to me was a very important issue. I brought up my concerns, and we resolved that we wouldn't take any more trips to Colorado until we had made a family trip to Virginia. Had I continued to hold onto my resentment, it would have only gotten worse, and would have become a wedge in our relationship. The sooner conflict is resolved, the sooner we can reinstate the happy in happy *ever after*.

To Yell or Not to Yell

I asked my mother once how she and my father raised such confident and successful children. She was flattered by the question but humble with her answer. She told me she truly believed it was because "our home was not a yelling home. We did not yell at each other, and we did not yell at the kids." To my parent's credit, it is true. Yelling was not a part of my childhood, and I think she is right. Yelling ushers peace and contentment right out the door.

In the heat of conflict, yelling is often one of our first responses. It can move people to act and at the same time move them to rebel. Unless you are in a life or death situation, yelling is a futile tool. Like blame, it doesn't solve problems, but it creates more tension. It makes one feel as if they are being attacked which in turn, turns on defense mechanisms. It escalates situations rather than resolving them.

When my family was trying to clean, the more we yelled, the more upset everyone became. I loathe yelling, and I despise how it makes me feel. I don't want my children or spouse to feel they must yell in order to be heard. I admit at times I find it difficult not to yell, but when I succeed, peace is restored in abundance.

As my wise mother-in-law puts it, "Yelling is the extension of your emotions when they are over-taxed." Sometimes, when the smallest things happen in your family, whether with spouse or children, it is as if the end of a fuse that has been burning for some time and your family gets the bomb. Focus on finding alternative diffusers for your bomb. Exercise, get some fresh air, or write in your journal. Don't allow your conflicts to be managed with yelling; it won't resolve your issues.

When I have reached my emotional limit, I find it best to close my mouth, turn off the body language, and walk away until I can trust myself with the tender emotions of my family. Words and actions cannot be taken back and so should be chosen with wisdom and love.

When one of my children was younger, I felt beyond my limits in dealing with her defiance. In a terrible moment, I snapped. I took her toy and broke it over my knee. I am usually rather mild in my interactions, and this turn of events sent her into a sobbing fit. After the fact, I was filled with remorse because I knew I could not undo what I had done. As I pondered this moment, I realized if I had stayed silent or avoided action for even ten seconds, the outcome would have been more positive. Instead of reacting to the situation like a crazy woman, I could have come up with an intentional discipline that was more fitting to the crime. It would likely have been an outcome I would have spent less time lamenting and one from which my daughter would have learned a good lesson. Instead, all she or I can recall is my anger and a broken toy.

Next time you have reached your emotional breaking point, close your mouth, turn off your body language, and walk away. This little exercise is not meant to avoid conflict, but rather to resolve conflict while remaining in control of yourself. It is a tool that can avoid years of heartache because it allows us the foresight to make better choices. The key, of course, is remembering to use it.

Choose Your Battles Wisely

Choose your battles wisely. My mother-in-law maintains, "If it is not a big deal, don't make it a big deal; if it is [a big deal], . . . make it [a big deal]." Some things are just not worth emotion and the time, but some things are, and we need to have the courage to address the bigger issues.

When my now brother-in-law was considering engagement to my sister, he was very concerned about how finances would affect their possible marriage. He would become worried or stressed every time she said something about going shopping, eating out, or spending any money at all. His concerns on this matter were valid, as he had come from a family which had fallen on very difficult financial times. Though his parents managed their money in many smart ways, their fiscal management did not prepare them for future financial strains. When unexpected medical expenses were added to existing debts, the stress caused tension in their marriage. My brother-in-law was afraid of having similar financial issues in his marriage and he and my sister began to have conflict over the very topic he feared. He says, "I remember one night when we sat in the car on a randomly selected road and discussed my fears. My girlfriend was really sensitive and I came to feel that she really understood why I was so scared and why spending habits were such a big deal to me. I realized that she didn't want to go into debt either and that she knew spending wisely was important. I came to understand that she had her own fears of missing out on opportunities because of being too stingy. We discussed specifics and found solutions we were both happy with." Neither of their spending habits was necessarily bad, but they were different and they needed to find common ground that he felt safe with and she felt comfortable with. He picked this battle because he wanted to have better than decent spending habits; he wanted to be ready for a rainy day. It was a battle wisely chosen, as it would have very likely become a raging conflict in their marriage. It improved their relationship by helping them to come together on an important issue and giving him the confidence to pop the question.

Next time you are choosing a battle, ask yourself if the battle will eventually help your relationships or hurt them. Spending habits can make or break a marriage, but does it really matter if your spouse wears mismatched socks? There is absolutely no way to avoid conflict, but everything isn't and doesn't need to be a conflict. Sometimes, it's okay to let things go.

There are so many things in need of my attention that sometimes letting things go means I simply shove my husband's clothes to his side of the bed until he gets tired of tripping on them. If I can't see them, I don't care, and for me, it's not worth arguing about. However, fighting for family time is important to me and worth the battle. If I don't get my date night, it's a problem because it hurts our relationship. Not every situation is urgent. Don't wander through your world looking for everything that is wrong. If there really is a conflict that needs resolving, you will likely know about it. If you really can't stand that your husband wears ugly shirts, that your wife tries to bring up important life topics after you are tucked in bed with the lights out, or that your kids squeeze toothpaste everywhere, bring it up. A good friend reminded me that our relationships should be strong enough that we can feel free to discuss the things that bother us. But even in the strongest relationships, voicing every dislike we have about our loved ones or every frustration we feel they are the cause of will eventually strain the relationship. It is not criticism or complaint that motivates change, but rather love. Don't waste your time and energy looking for battles to fight. You will always find one, and you will always be fighting.

Forgiveness

We have previously mentioned the power of forgiveness in our familial relationships, but I find it important to reiterate and expand. We cannot reasonably discuss conflict resolution without discussing forgiveness. Resolving conflict means we apologize, but what is harder than that is that we must forgive. When I was pregnant with our first child, my husband was telling me a story as we waited in line at a wedding reception. I kept interrupting him with questions in order to be sure I was following. He became so fed up with my interruptions he told me to shut up. I could not believe he could be so rude to me, and in public, too. I was angry and hurt, and even though it was probably the first mean thing he had ever said to me, the night was ruined.

In our agony, we waited in silence to give our best wishes to the bride and groom. We didn't stay to chat with old friends, but practically ran out of the reception. Later on, knowing how much his words hurt me, my husband was groveling in his sincere desire to apologize. I was still wondering how he could be so mean. He really tried to show his sorrow for his rash comment. The only way to let it go was to forgive him and move on.

Far more hurtful things and meaner words and actions take place in families than a simple "shut up." Deep wounds and conflicts will arise on your path to *ever after*, but that is how journeys are. There are always bumps and potholes but the road doesn't end unless we choose to end it. No matter how great the offense is, we cannot possibly resolve conflict, improve trust, and move on with a happy life if we are not willing to forgive each other or ourselves.

For some reason, we as humans grasp onto anger, hurt, and sadness as if they are lifelines. We hold on to them because we're afraid we will be losing something if we don't simmer a little longer. Maybe we fear our pride is at stake or that forgiveness will make us vulnerable. The real truth, however, is that when we hang onto the conflicts, hurt, and anger, we lose happiness and love.

To the Critic of Love

One morning after my shower, I noticed my bed was made. I asked my husband if he was the one who made it. He replied, "Yes," and I in turn replied with, "Thank you." Disappointed that I did not fall down at his feet with gratitude, he persisted to talk about it. My sister was visiting at the time, and so my husband asked me what I would have said to her had she been the one to make the bed. I was starting to catch on to the fact that this was a test and I realized my husband was expecting a response he wasn't getting. I laughed and said, "I would have said thank you. There is just one difference between you and her. You actually slept in the bed."

I learned later on that my husband was feeling like I had been treating my extended family better than him, my sister included. I was so grateful I took the time to appreciate his efforts and let the Red Punch Experiment work on our marriage for good. However, I was bothered by the fact he felt like he was doing me a favor by making our bed. I felt like he should feel just as much responsibility to make it as I did.

After a while I brought up the situation again, but this time I was on a mission to convince him I was right and that he needed to change. I began to see him as a chauvinist and an unthoughtful man. "I am not your servant!" I maintained. He began to fight back and started to see me as ungrateful and unreasonable. He felt he worked so long and hard for me that the least I could do was make the bed because I was usually still in it when he left, which is true.

As I watched his calm, loving aura become darkened, I realized I was destroying our precious time together. My telling him to change was not going to change anything. I altered my approach and said with sincere love, "It's really hard sometimes when we have such different beliefs on how our home life should be." I let all of my anger go and vicious thoughts evaporate. I loved him, even if he didn't make the bed.

The next morning I walked in my room to find my husband making the bed. There was no sarcasm or cutting remarks, only love. I don't know if this change came because he believed I was right or if it was simply because he cared how I felt, but it meant the world to me because I knew his actions were motivated by love.

It is hard to take the higher road. It takes more time, patience, humility, and love, but it is the only path that will inspire lasting change and resolution. Do we love, revere, and look up to the parent, spouse, or family member who swears at us, belittles us, and constantly throws grenades at our armor? It is unlikely. The parent or spouse who shows us respect and love, even when they do not agree with us, has a far greater reach into our hearts. They are the ones who inspire change. They are the ones we look up to, they are the ones we want to be a part of our *ever after*.

Sometimes we come across a rotten egg in our nests, and no matter how much love we give them or how many Red Punch Experiments we use on them, they crack and it stinks! If you find this to be the case after sincere effort on your part, it might be appropriate to seek professional counseling. Love your family members safely. It is not necessary or healthy to let them hurt you or other family members. When people "stink" the most, this is often the time when they need the most love. Stand beside them and support them. Let them know you love them. Fight for your family, but do not stoop to their level.

Resolving conflict involves listening with love and understanding. This doesn't always mean agreeing. We shouldn't force our beliefs and ideas on anyone, even our spouse and children. There have been a few occasions when my husband's beliefs and my beliefs were so different and immovable we had to agree to disagree while still maintaining our love.

We will all have moments when we are wrong. We need to base the outcomes of our conflict resolution on truth, not pride. If we are wrong or there is a better way than our way, it is okay to admit it. If perchance our spouse or children admit to being wrong, we should not gloat. We are not weak when we show love or extend forgiveness, and our relationships will be strengthened by our willingness to compromise and try to understand another's way of doing things.

My wise grandmother reiterated, "Occasionally we shout, or are wrong in how we resolve conflict, but if our loved ones know we love them, it will compensate. Love is overpowering and essential. We all make mistakes and need to ask for forgiveness. Build a foundation of love your family can stand on and feel firm on. You still love them and it's okay." Love really is a powerful thing. Let it be your guide to finding peace in conflict resolution.

CHAPTER EIGHT

Great Expectations

Challenge: Have a family counsel

As I awoke from a not-so-restful sleep, my mind turned to the day ahead. I had already created my well-thought-out, clear schedule, and I was preparing for its perfect execution. There was to be precision, cooperation, and speed by all family members. I was going to wake up at 5 a.m., work out, write a new chapter in my book, shower and get dressed, make a tasty and heart-warming breakfast for the family, get the kitchen cleaned up, and maybe clean the bathroom by 7 a.m. Then, I planned to wake up the kids. They would get dressed without any moaning, practice piano, do the rest of their homework for the week, make lunches, and eat breakfast together. My husband would help with the breakfast dishes, water that dead spot on the lawn, and drop the car off for an oil change. Then we would all part ways at 8:30 a.m. with hugs and kisses to go about our day.

My beautiful plan would have worked out if it weren't for the plans everyone else had already made. To my dismay, my husband wanted to sleep in because he stayed up late watching a movie—how irresponsible. The kids had to be pushed out of bed and reminded every five minutes that skipping school wasn't an option and I really would make them go in their pajamas.

My threats fell on deaf ears as the kids were more enthralled with Jackson's new motorized dump truck and its lifelike engine sounds. They were neither interested nor motivated by my perfect plan that would indeed make everyone's life wonderful. Practicing the piano was far from their minds. They expected me to make their lunches, and they figured their homework wasn't due until Friday, so why do it now?

When my husband rolled out of bed, he had his own plans that did not involve dishes and lawn watering. He did plan to change the oil in his truck, but not in my car. He had to send invoices, check emails, and run off to meet some employees before he could even sample my homemade breakfast. My perfectly executed plan crumbled, and before the day was in full swing, I was already feeling unsatisfied and discouraged, thinking, "Why can't they just do what I expect?"

Often, we trick ourselves with the idea of perfection. We plan our family's time down to the second and expect that our agenda is everyone else's agenda. A more realistic scenario for my morning would be to roll out of bed at 7:00 a.m., hurry to wake the kids, fight for bathroom time, dine on gourmet cereal, hand out lunch money, and remember to lock the door on the way out.

Tired of the contention created every morning by my unfulfilled expectations, I simply decided it was my kids' responsibility to get up and get ready for school. I could not afford to let it be my problem. By this, I do not imply that I don't need to take responsibility for my children, but that it simply wasn't worth the stress, yelling, or tears to enforce this routine. I told the kids I would pay them five dollars a semester to be ready and on time for school. For every tardy, they would lose one dollar. I stopped fighting, and I left it at that.

Something amazing happened. We all began to enjoy the mornings, even when we didn't get what we hoped for. The kids still wasted oodles of time, and I patiently reminded myself that it wasn't my problem. I no longer enforced my expectations with the sword. The kids knew what was expected and it became worth it to them. Sometimes they did it and sometimes they didn't do it, but our home became a happier place because I let them be.

We all have visions and make plans for how we want our family to be and our home to be run, for the kind of house we want to live in, the food we eat, and the activities we are involved in. These ideals are fantastic, but problems arise when our vision of life does not match that of the ones we love and live with. They arise when we or our family cannot possibly meet the expectations we have so innocently fashioned. They arise when our expectations are entirely unrealistic, one-sided, or just plain impossible. The great expectations of our lives can make for depressing *ever afters.* Our expectations can clutter up and inhibit our roller-coaster car and keep us from obtaining our dreams.

Hoping for things, having goals, and creating dreams for our family and ourselves will always be an important component to successful, happy families. We must remember, however, to keep our hopes and visions realistic and be willing to bounce back from disappointment and unmet expectations because there will be many of them.

The first Thanksgiving my husband and I spent together turned out to be one vast unmet expectation for me. We had traveled to be with his family and we were both excited. We lived far away from extended family and looked forward to the reunion. After we said our hellos and hugged everyone, my husband disappeared. I had hoped we would be together for this vacation, and the longer he was gone playing with his brothers, the more impatient I became. As we sat down for our highly anticipated feast, I was disappointed with the paper plates and appalled that people were leaving the table unceremoniously and at will.

There is nothing wrong with the way they did Thanksgiving, except it was not what I had expected. I became homesick for a beautifully set table with Grandma's old china and the tradition of everyone reminiscing about the things they were thankful for throughout the year.

I spent the next evening alone. My husband stayed up late into the night playing video games with his cousins and brothers while I was confined to the bathroom, where I was dealing with the sudden onset of the stomach flu. I was miserable and upset that my husband wasn't taking care of me. He should have tied my hair back, brought me a Coke, and entertained me while I nibbled on soda crackers.

These situations were not errors or mistakes, but learning experiences for both of us. Because we had never shared a Thanksgiving together, I was entirely unprepared for his family's style. It was wrong of me to expect his family to use glass plates and have everyone sit at the table until everyone else had finished. Their family is different than mine and there is nothing wrong with that. When it came to being sick, my husband admitted he didn't know I expected any of the treatment I so desired. I never told him I was sick, and he assumed I was sleeping. Though I supposed it was obvious, we had never discussed my expectation for him to spend time with me or his expectation to spend time with his brothers, whom he missed very much. I realized quickly that my needs and desires were not the only needs and desires worth considering.

Imagine how it makes our families feel when they know they do not live up to our awesome expectations. Imagine the extra tension we create in ourselves and our family each morning when we realize that against our will, the bathroom is not going to get cleaned, the dishes will be left undone, and the kids really do plan on going to school in their pajamas. It is exhausting and depressing. We need to pay attention to how our expectations affect the people around us. No one wants to spend time in a world where they can never possibly be the person we think they should be or do the things we expect them to do. I admit it is annoying at times to have to let go of my expectations to allow someone else to have their own expectations, but that's what families do. When I visit my parents, I expect to spend quality time with them, just as my husband expects to spend quality time with his brothers when he visits them. If we find ourselves always at odds with the people we should love and enjoy most, it may be time to honestly evaluate the reality of our expectations.

Allowing Personality while Maintaining Expectation

Any parent can attest to the fact that children come with personalities already in place. Trying to get your spouse or your children to be carbon copies of you, your ideals, or your desires is unrealistic. However, as parents, this does not mean we give into every whim or desire of our children or that we allow them to go against our morals or beliefs. If we were to let our children develop their own beliefs based on what they see on TV and learn in school without any guidance, discipline, moral bearing, or healthy expectations, our society would be brimming with a misguided, selfish, and irresponsible populace. Children can maintain their personalities and we as parents can remain in charge.

As an example, my Ella hates having her hair done by me or anyone else, but as a parent I feel like it is my job to teach her proper hygiene for many reasons, and so I expect her to do her hair every day, even when she doesn't want to. Personally, I love updos or curly locks, but she is content with a ponytail. As long as her ponytail is clean and neat, she can have a ponytail every day. She doesn't need curly locks to have good hygiene. As parents, we have the responsibility to teach our children what is important to us, help them develop a sense of right and wrong, and teach them attributes and qualities that will allow them to formulate and develop their own ideas and beliefs.

When it comes to our spouse, aside from realizing that we just have different personalities, it is vital to remember how different men and women are genetically. The longer I am married, the more I can appreciate our differences. We think differently and we respond to life differently. We expect different things. My husband loves a good argument and truly enjoys trying to persuade me. He wants me to think like him and respond as he would respond. It took me years to convince him that we could be unified as a couple but still have our own ideas and opinions while continuing to be happy and have a loving relationship.

We recently had an account discrepancy at the bank and it was looking like it was going to be problematic. Not wanting the stress of resolving the situation myself, I passed the baton to my husband. I wanted him to call the bank immediately, but he decided to wait until the next day and go to the bank in person. When he went to the bank, it appeared everything was fine, but I was not satisfied. I felt like he needed to be more detailed in his inquiry, so I pushed him to call and talk with the bank again. He was upset. He expected me to trust that he had taken care of things and I expected he would be more thorough. This brought up an interesting point. My husband felt that if I wasn't pleased with what he had done, then I should take care of things myself. This, of course, annoyed me just enough to hang up on him and do it myself. He was pleased that he had ruffled my feathers enough to throw me into action, and it was soon revealed that everything was fine, just as he said.

Part of family life is allowing people to do things their way. After our little bank adventure, we made a deal that when my husband takes care of something, he gets to do it his way, and when I do something, I get to take care of it my way, and neither of us can complain about the other person's way of doing things. We also agreed that if something really wasn't working and was actually important (like how we raise our children) then we would re-evaluate together as to how our expectations need to change.

When we were first married, both my husband and I were still in college. I was on a quick, solid path to graduation. All my classes were scheduled and I had already worked out any kinks. I expected my husband to have done the same. When he said he had two more years left, I believed him. During those two years, I was patient, but when the next year came and went, I exploded like a firework: "How could you not have planned this out?"

It became important to reevaluate our expectations because it was having a negative impact on our family and future. Needless to say, it was shortly after that that he visited a counselor, planned an actual graduation date, and yes, graduated. Because I had my entire college career calculated and planned out, I assumed and expected that he had done the same, and when I realized he hadn't, I was upset. He wasn't upset that he didn't have a plan, but I was. If I would have just talked to him about it years earlier and asked him to make a plan, he probably would have done it. He wasn't defiant about it, but he just didn't know I expected it.

This example illustrates an important point. When it comes to our expectations, we cannot assume anything. I assumed he would be more organized and he assumed I didn't care, so it became a problem. We need to be careful not to assume our spouse, children, or parents know how we feel about something. It is highly unlikely our families will be able to read between the lines, and we shouldn't expect them to. We also shouldn't assume that when we sweetly express our desires and expectations, our family will suddenly agree and act accordingly.

When we expect our spouse or children to respond in certain ways or make certain choices, we need to ask ourselves if we have clearly communicated with them or told them our wishes. Then, we need to bite our tongues and let them discover their agency and its consequences, or we need to realize they simply don't want to do things our way.

Our expectations are often selfish and can inhibit our ability to improve ourselves and our family because we think our way is better. These expectations can keep us from really enjoying some of life's best unexpected moments. Sometimes, we think our way is faster or more efficient, but that doesn't mean it's always better. When I do the dishes, my way is definitely faster and more efficient then my husband's way. He likes to get comfortable, have a snack, and watch a movie while doing dishes. It used to make me crazy because it turned a fifteen-minute job into an hour-and-seventeen-minute job. I just wanted him to get it done so we could move onto whatever was next on my list. He could not have cared less about my list and was going to have fun while he did the dishes. I finally learned it really was just fine for him to have a movie and dishes night. The outcome took longer, but the dishes still got done and my husband was much happier as a result.

I had to let go of my expectation that everyone would use and appreciate my efficient dish cleaning system for the good of the whole. We are a family, and as such, must work with differing opinions, ideas, and ways of doing things. We need to be certain we aren't assuming and instead we must communicate with each other concerning our desires. We need to work with everyone's expectations, not just our own.

Evaluate Reality

My husband owns an electrical company, so he never has set working hours. As you have previously discovered about me, I like to map out life, and his work schedule is not conducive to such planning. For years, I would make plans and expect him to be home. Every time I had to send the babysitter away because he didn't show up for date night, I would get so upset. He would defend himself, saying he couldn't change his work schedule. He had to finish his jobs and he had to meet his deadlines. He was right, but I had great expectations for our family and it was hard for me to modify them. This caused a lot of contention for us because I would be upset or hurt that he let down my expectations, and he would feel guilty or be upset that my expectations were impossible for him to meet. It was a terrible cycle.

I don't know when it happened, but one day I discovered that it was my expectations causing these problems and I realized it's hard to be disappointed if you don't have any expectations. Suddenly my mind-set changed. If he said he was going to be home at 5:00 p.m., I hoped he would be home by 8 p.m.. If he called me and said he couldn't make it to an event, I went by myself and I was happy to do it. This did two things for us. First, the contention was gone. Second, he tried harder to be home for things because he knew I was going to go anyway.

Notice the norms in your family and, instead of always fighting against them, try to find ways to work with them. I still make plans and I still enjoy eating dinner with my husband, but I still mentally assume he will be home two hours later than when he says he will be home. I can't change his work schedule—believe me, I've tried—but a slight alteration in my expectations has made our journey so much more fun.

Around the same time as this frustration with my husband's work schedule was happening, I would get frustrated or depressed because I began to expect that my husband was going to let me down, based on his history. This was infuriating to my husband. He would say he was "getting in trouble for things he hadn't done yet." Honestly, it was true. My expectations had been dashed so many times that I began planning for it. Interestingly, I again thought it was always my husband who was letting me down, and never that I was expecting too much. Well, it is quite apparent that I was wrong. Unsurprisingly, my husband does want to be with our family. He loves coming home for dinner and eating it while it is still warm. It seems a little silly now that I knew my expectations weren't going to be fulfilled, but I still expected them.

I have found realism to be very beneficial. My experience has taught me that the best solution for me is to continue to plan and have hope in plans, but be willing to go with the flow when they must change. Hope is vital in families, and I am definitely not advocating for poor planning, depression, or even just giving into situations. I'm simply reminding you that situations will always be changing, so be careful about what you expect and be willing to change.

For every family, situations are different, but the idea is the same. Maybe you expected to have more or less kids. Maybe you expected to make more money and have a nicer house. Maybe you expected your child to become the valedictorian. Maybe you expected your husband to mow the lawn, or your wife to have the laundry done. Maybe you didn't expect to be single. It is great to have goals. It is great to plan, but you must plan on life happening, and life has a way of changing the best plans.

Be Proactive

As we sat down to the dinner table, I realized I didn't have a fork. Just as I was about to ask my daughter, who already had a fork and was sitting next to me, to get one for me, I stopped. I had no ailments, I wasn't hurt or in need, so why was I asking my daughter to get the fork for me? I knew I shouldn't, and in that moment, I clearly recalled numerous occasions I had lectured my children saying, "If you are not willing to do something for yourself when you are capable of doing it, then you shouldn't expect someone else to do it for you." I had to eat my own words, and I stood and walked the short distance to get myself a fork. I was reminded that a family is a team and should help one another. There is nothing wrong with serving our loved ones. Through our service to one another, we can learn the importance of selfless giving, but we should not abuse that service with demands and expectations. If you can do it for yourself, you should do it.

It is important that we take responsibility for ourselves and that we teach our children to take responsibility for themselves. As parents, we should teach our children this responsibility of serving and taking care of themselves through our own actions. This seems like common sense, but I can't tell you how many times I sent my children to go clean the bathroom, not for any reason other than I just didn't want to do it. I really loathe cleaning the bathroom. I loathe it so much I am willing to accept a half done job just so I don't have to do it. I finally felt guilty that I always made my kids do the job I hated. I repented and started helping the kids clean the bathroom—now we all share the responsibility. I needed to lead by example.

Along these same lines, we shouldn't wait for others to do things for us that we can do ourselves. At our house, it is my husband's job to take the trash out to the street every Tuesday morning. On rare occasions, as he is running out the door, taking the trash out slips his mind. I get so annoyed by this, and sometimes in my stubbornness, I am even tempted to let the trash rot and overflow for another week. When I realize I too will suffer from such a choice and that I am quite capable of lugging the trash to the street, I begin to question my expectations. I ask myself if it is really so important for my husband to take out the trash. I remember that he is just as busy as I am, and I am so appreciative when he helps me out. I also think to myself that once the trash is gone, I don't have to be upset about it anymore.

On another occasion, I waited for months for my husband to build a desk for my daughter so that she would have a place to do her work. The longer I felt my request was ignored, the more upset I became. I finally let go of the expectation I had for him to build it, and I built it myself. I definitely did not do as good of a job as my husband would have done, but the desk is still standing and I am quite proud of it. Both my husband and I are happy that I am no longer bugging him to build a desk, and my daughter is happy she has a place to do her work.

I had been pleading with my husband to fix the flat tire on my double stroller, as it was my lifeline to the outside world. The longer I had to wait for it, the more impatient I became. One afternoon, my husband and I were discussing the matter when I began to giggle. I felt a little guilty as I admitted to my husband that I did in fact know how to change the tire but just didn't want to. My husband was less than amused, knowing I could have fixed it all along while I had been upset at him for not doing it.

On all of these occasions, I could have been angry or bitter at my husband for not meeting my expectations. However, they were my expectations and I had the capability to fulfill them. My husband did fix the stroller, even though I was capable of doing it. The desk would have been nicer if he had built it. The trash will always stink if I leave it. The point is, I am usually happier when I work to fulfill my own expectations than when I wait for someone else to do it for me.

Obviously, we should use a different approach with our children than we do with our spouse. With our children, our expectations need to include teaching and following up. We shouldn't always pick up the slack for our children or they will not learn responsibility. When I was twelve, in my excitement to go over to my friends, I attempted to thwart my job to take out the trash. About an hour after I ditched my job for more exciting options, my dad showed up at my friend's house and took me home so I could take out the trash. My dad expected me to do my job and taught me an important lesson about responsibility. A few years later, when I was playing high school sports and involved in choir, theatre, and numerous other activities, my parents maintained their expectations but also allowed me a little more freedom. As I juggled my time, they were patient when I waited until Saturday to clean the bathroom or mow the lawn. My parents often found opportunities to quietly ease my burden and show their love for me. I provide both of these examples because, as parents, we need to remember that our children sometimes need a break just like we do. We need times when it is okay not to be perfect.

My kids are sweet and usually willing to run my little errands, but I shouldn't make them do them or let them clean the bathroom on their own, just because I don't like it. We all need to do our part in the home. Waiting for others to do things we don't want to do, feel are not our responsibility, or are intimidated by doesn't bring peace. Having the smelly trash rot outside my house would not have made me happier, but having it gone, whether I took it to the street or Bryce did, does make me happy. If my daughter's desk still wasn't built, you can be certain I would be agonizing over it and continue to be upset at my husband, but now I just enjoy the desk because I took the time to build it. As we take responsibility for our own expectations and ourselves, our homes will be happier places to be.

When the Going Gets Tough . . . the Tough Should Slow Down

As the temperatures dropped and the snow swirled around our car, I began holding my breath, only to catch myself taking a gulp a few seconds later. The winter storm was upon us in full fury as we drove across the barren plains of Wyoming. I could only hope my tires were up to the slushy and icy challenge. As the storm intensified, we chose to slow down and be more cautious. We knew that at our current speed, which was the speed meant for perfect weather, we had little traction and little control. We watched, horrified, as a truck flew by us and plummeted straight into the snow bank, followed by another car driving too fast for the weather conditions. After making sure the people in both vehicles were okay, we continued because our minivan was incapable of pulling them out. We knew it was going to take longer to get to our destination at our turtle speed, but unlike the many cars nestled in the snow banks around us, we would make it to our destination long before they would.

Whenever the storms of our life roll in, we can only hope we are prepared with good traction on our tires, lots of windshield wiper fluid, and functional wipers. However, even when we are as prepared as we can be, sometimes we must slow down and even alter our course. If we had continued our journey at full speed in such uncertain and stressful conditions, I have no doubt that we would have crashed or become stuck like the many cars around us. Life is not always filled with sunshine and blue skies and when we try to race through as if nothing has changed, we often find ourselves crashing, burning, and taking longer to arrive at our desired destination than we would have if we had just slowed down.

There are days, weeks, and months when even the lowest expectations are hard to maintain. These are likely the moments when we walk around in a haze, telling ourselves we can do it, and murmuring under our breath, "I hate my life." There is nothing wrong with letting some of our expectations slide until we can regain traction and control.

For my Aunt Sandy the haze set in when her family welcomed twin boys. Some days, just getting food in her children's mouth was literally all she could do. The older kids could help, but the house and yard could not be maintained with the same level of cleanliness that it had before. She felt like she barely had time to maintain herself. Extracurricular activities waned and there were less family outings. Laundry . . . well there was heaps of it. With six children to take care of, how could there not be? To drastically understate the situation, life was hard. This family's blue sky was dim. As Sandy and her family trimmed down their expectations, they were able to make it through a difficult time without the family falling apart.

When there are major life changes or high stress, it is not wise to run at the same pace and hold on to the same expectations that we may have had previously. The stress, frustration, desperation, and depression that constantly knock at the door will run rampant in our lives if we don't slow down or alter our course. Our child can miss one baseball season and, despite what others say, we are not bad parents and our children are not being neglected. It is okay to say we are not going to do piano this month. We do not need to attend every event we are invited to, and it's okay to take a day off work. We need to find ways to make life manageable and stop expecting ourselves to be at peak performance every day. Just as my parents were aware and patient in my overwhelming high school days, we also should be considerate and aware of our family as they experience overwhelming periods in their life. Expecting them to maintain certain levels of performance could be unhealthy and unwise, and may lead to a total wipeout.

Two Wrongs Don't Make a Right

Sometimes, when our expectations are let down by the people we love, we become hurt and disappointed. We may use this disappointment as an excuse for us to make choices that are just as unthoughtful and hurtful. We shouldn't let our unmet expectations be an excuse for us to do wrong, be unkind, or become a victim. Two wrongs don't make a right. Instead, we should try to treat our family kindly and help them fulfill their expectations. Choose to treat your family better than your friends and associates, not so much because they've earned that love or deserve it, but because it is the right thing to do.

When my daughter came home from school one day, she was so sad. One of her friends was continually making unkind and petty remarks to her and about her. When other kids would come and play with this friend, she would tell my daughter to go away. When my daughter told me this, my first advice was to tell her to send her friend packing. Subliminally, I added, "Dish it back to her." If she is not going to play with you, don't play with her. This, however, did not ease my daughter's tears, so I tried a different approach.

I asked her if she could think of a reason why this might be happening, if she had done or said anything unkind herself. She couldn't think of anything, so I counseled her to invite her friend over to make cupcakes and beaded necklaces. Her friend accepted the offer and the girls had a wonderful time. After their playdate, the mean words stopped and they were fast friends again.

My daughter had expected her friend to do the sort of things good friends do, like be kind and play with her. When my daughter's friend let down her expectations, I advised my daughter to no longer be a good friend by ending the relationship. I felt justified in this because her friend wasn't being good to her and I don't want to encourage my daughter to build relationships with people who willfully hurt her. However, had she taken my first counsel, the relationship would have ended and likely the unkind remarks would have persisted. Because my daughter continued to treat her friend as she expected friends should be treated, the friendship was healed.

Just as my daughter took the higher road with her friend, we should do the same with our loved ones. We shouldn't hesitate to buy a box of chocolates for our spouse because they never buy us sweet treats, or avoid buying surprise tickets to the Bronco's game because our spouse never surprises us. We shouldn't avoid writing a sweet note and dropping it in their lunch box, because they don't write us sweet notes. We can still make it a point to complement our spouse or children when we receive no such praise from them. Don't evade doing something kind for your spouse or your children with the excuse they never do the kind things for you that you expect.

If you are feeling like your expectations are never being met, it is okay, appropriate, and important to discuss these unmet expectations with your spouse or children. Taking the higher road doesn't mean you must become a martyr or live in hurtful conditions. If my daughter's friend persisted in being unkind to her, I would still counsel her to stay away from her, but I would expect my daughter not to return the cutting remarks or be mean in any way. If as a family we take the time to discuss and share our expectations, even about the littlest things like how we expect a kiss before bed, want breakfast in bed for our birthday, or would rather eat pancakes than waffles, it will be much easier for our family to help fulfill those expectations.

Family Council

A family council is the perfect platform to discuss our expectations. Start by making a comprehensive list of your expectations for you, your spouse, and your children for one week. Then, ask them to make a list of their expectations for you and for themselves. Sit down together and evaluate your lists. Talk about what is most important to each of you, and then try to make it work. If you want your husband to fix the sink, this is the time to tell him. If he doesn't have time that day, ask him to pick a time that works for him or tell him you would like to hire a plumber. It is likely that not every expectation on everyone's list is going to be fulfilled. Pay attention to things that seem excessive or unrealistic and do away with them. Repeat this every week and over time you and your family will have a better idea of each other's expectations, and you will have less disappointment and more time for the things that bring happiness.

My family and I do our version of family counsel every Sunday afternoon. It is an open forum for us to share

136　　　　F a m i l y　E v e r　A f t e r

and align our schedules and expectations. We discuss work, school, play, house projects, new items we want to purchase, and whatever other needs and desires we have.

As we learn of the expectations and schedules in our families, it is important that we do our part to help everyone fulfill their expectations, within reason. Always remember the Red Punch Experiment. Show love and respect for the ones you love the most. If your friend needed help, you would probably help them, even if you didn't want to. Give that same gift, with all the love you can, to your own family.

My family had the opportunity to act on this principle after the birth of our fourth child. I lost control of the quickly mounting laundry pile, and we would wake up and have to dig through mounds of unfolded clothes to get ready for school, work, and life. We would spend our precious morning minutes matching socks and ironing clothes. My kids hated this and so did my husband. It especially irritated him that he couldn't find his socks. As my family expressed their need and expectation to have folded clothes, I tried to make it a point to conquer the laundry and they made it a point to help. Every time the clean pile of clothes stacked up, we would all sit down together, watch a movie, fold and put away clothes. I didn't love it because I don't love laundry, but everyone's efforts made it possible to meet my family's expectation for clean, folded, and put away clothes.

We can improve our family by paying attention to expectations, evaluating them, and taking action, just as my family did with our overabundant laundry pile. Life is not perfect. There will be days when the dishes don't get done, the dry cleaning never arrives at the dry cleaner, and the lawn is left to suffocate in the weeds. There will be days when our families will embarrass us, and it is okay. We shouldn't let our expectations be so great that it takes away from our family. Our goals, hopes, and expectations should add to the happiness of our life and that of our families.

I remember sitting down to dinner one night and eating something I really hated. It made me want to vomit. I looked around at my kids, who were eating it because I expected them to. As they carefully voiced their displeasure, I finally listened to them. You can be sure I choked down that meal and never made it again. Sometimes our expectations blind us, until we are forced to face the reality of the expectations we have created. I expected my kids to eat something even I hated. The next time my kids really hated what I made, I was a little more compassionate, paid closer attention to their likes and dislikes, and asked them what they would like.

Let's not waste our *ever after* buried under our excessive expectations. It only leads to resentment, anger, and depression, not just for us, but for our loved ones as well. We need to be more realistic with our expectations by noticing the norms of our family life and working with them. We need to avoid letting our unmet expectations be a chance to do things we know we shouldn't and we need to make sure we don't assume our family knows what we expect. We shouldn't expect our families to do things for us when we are capable of doing them ourselves. We should take the time to discuss and realize the expectations of our family and try to fulfill them if we can. Only then can we can enjoy the freedom and love that is found under our heaps of expectations. We can still be happy, even when our expectations are not always met. And I would venture to say we will be even happier when we focus more on the expectations of our loved ones than ourselves.

CHAPTER NINE

We Grow Funny Looking Cucumbers

... but they still taste good

Challenge: Pay attention to something a family member needs, and do it for them

Positive Patience

The more children I had, the more tired and impatient I became. I remember wondering, as I raised my voice at the kids for the millionth time, "What has happened to me? I used to have so much patience and so much joy in my crazy life." In an inspirational moment I figured it out. I had the same amount of patience I always had, it was just being stretched four times further and in hundreds of different directions. This was a much-needed epiphany because I felt corrupted by my lack of patience. I would tell myself, "You used to be so nice—such a good parent and spouse—and now look at you." Maybe it sounds dramatic, but it really saddened me. As I gained a glimpse of reality, and myself, I began working on increasing my patience to allow for the load I carried. I needed to find a way to enjoy my *ever after* even when I felt like a frayed rubber band.

Increasing my patience and enjoying my continuously outlandish life as a wife and mother has been an ongoing process with constant adjustments. I was enjoying lunch with my grandparents one afternoon. In preparation for our meal, my grandma was peeling some oddly shaped cucumbers she had grown in her garden. As we laughed at their appearance my grandma said, "We grow funny looking cucumbers, but they still taste good." Just like our cucumbers, family life can be a little crazy and unexpected, but it can still "taste" good and bring happiness when we lose ourselves in positive thinking, laugh, serve our loved ones, create special occasions, and make our house a home.

Lose Yourself in Positive Thinking

There is immense power in positive thinking. When I was in elementary school we had an assembly featuring a guest speaker. I don't remember his name or what his profession was, but he changed my life. He told us, when someone asks him how he is doing he always responds, "I'm doing great." He said when he first began this exercise he didn't actually feel great, but after voicing a heartfelt, "I'm doing great," he began to believe it and he began to feel it. My sixth-grade-self took that advice to heart and every time someone asked me how I was doing, I told them I was great!

The challenge soon began working its magic on me, and I started to feel and believe I was doing great. My childhood woes didn't seem as overwhelming. I started focusing more on others instead of myself. I attribute this to the fact that I felt my life was so "great," I didn't need to worry about me. As a rule of thumb I began to look for the positive things in other people and life in general. I began to have more friends and, although I was still a tween, I could see a huge difference in myself. A few years later when my mom volunteered my services to babysit without asking my permission, I was happy to help, and I knew it was because of this one change I had made years earlier. I was happy to serve because I was doing great! I had no reason not to help.

Through the years, life has become much harder and I noticed as my family has grown I no longer reply "I'm doing great." I became lost somewhere in the, "I'm okay but tired" haze. The less great I told people I was doing, the less great I felt. I found less happiness and became more selfish. As I began to reuse this great advice, even when my responsibilities are greater and stress is magnified—in the middle of raising kids, and still aiming to be a wonderful wife—the principle still works. It fills my patience reserve and helps me to truly be happy. There is immense power in being positive.

As a close friend of mine was attending school for psychology, his class did a little experiment. They put a bracelet on their wrist and every time they complained or said something negative, they had to move the bracelet to the other wrist, keeping track of the amount of times they changed it. It was very enlightening for him to see how negative he really was. It was the perfect eye opener to gain insight into his happiness level, and I suggest you give it a try.

Get yourself a bracelet or rubber band and put it on your wrist for one day. Move the bracelet to the opposite wrist each time you are negative. Keep track of the number of times you move it. Then take it a step further. The next day, put your lovely arm jewelry back on and only move it when you say positive things. Keep track of the number of times you change it from wrist to wrist. Take note of how you are feeling. Make a list of all the good things that have happened to you that day and post it somewhere you can see it. Make it a goal for the next week to always respond, "I'm doing great!" At the end of the week do the bands again, and see how you are feeling. Be especially positive about your family life and loved ones.

If we want to enjoy our families and find that extra bit of patience that will make our *ever after* amazing, we need to be more positive. Being positive might just give us the ability to better utilize the Red Punch Experiment. When that glass of Kool-Aid spills it might help us remember that we love our family more than the mess and stain left on the floor. Maybe we could make it a good memory rather than a woe. No one wants to live in an environment or home filled with negativity. It is hard on morale, hard on self-esteem, and hard on love.

Laugh

When I hear my two-year-old's deep, rolling laughter it engulfs me with delight. No matter what ails me, it brings me joy. Laughter is miraculous. It can change moods, relieve stress, calm tension, create bonds, and build our capability to stretch our patience. In the midst of many escalating moments in our family, we have been able to abruptly change direction when one of the kids says something funny. Instead of pursuing the argument, we laugh.

This happened one night when we enjoyed taco salad for dinner. We were in the process of cleaning up when my son brought the salsa from the table and carelessly emptied it onto the counter and floor. We chuckled a bit as we all worked together to clean it up. He promptly returned to the table, grabbed the bag of shredded cheese by the bottom and dumped it out across the table, chairs, floor and then counter. I could see it all happen but wasn't quick enough to stop the destruction. The contents of the now empty bag of cheese were staggered throughout the kitchen.

Oddly, my immediate reaction was to laugh, wondering how could he be so clumsy, but as I comprehended his carelessness and the new mess, we would again have to clean up, I withheld my snicker, and could feel my frustration rise. I began an internal battle with myself. "Do I pursue resolution with laughter or anger?" I was leaning towards getting mad. As I let my frustration envelop the situation, Daniel, as well as our happiness, retreated. Even in this moment, I knew if I could just laugh about the emptied bag of cheese, the situation would have a quicker and happier resolution. In the end, I knew whether I yelled or laughed, taught him or made demands, the cheese would get cleaned up. My actions would only affect my stress level, the feeling in the home, and the way I made my kids feel. I decided, by some miracle, that I would rather handle the situation with laughter than anger. As I again began to laugh, I was able to extend my patience and be kind about the situation. My laughter even enabled my son to crack a smile, and together we went back to the kitchen to clean up the cheese, and discussed ways that he could avoid making such messes in the future.

In another similar situation (also involving cheese) we had the opportunity to let laughter bring joy. As my husband and I were relishing a Sunday afternoon nap, we suddenly heard our two oldest children screaming "Fire!" There are few things that can persuade a parent to move faster. We bolted to the dining room to discover our children jumping from couch, to chair, to floor, throwing handfuls of shredded cheese through the air and screaming "Fire!" We walked backed to our room, locked the door, and laughed until we could laugh no more. After we gained control of ourselves, we returned to the kitchen, put away the remainder of the cheese, and gave a little lecture on wasting food. We had the kids help us clean up the explosion of cheese and then taught them a lesson on the seriousness of yelling fire and the boy who cried wolf. This is one of the moments in my children's lives that I am so grateful I enjoyed with laughter rather than anger. We can allow appropriate laughter to permeate and improve almost any situation.

Many families who have experienced traumatic events can find joy and peace through laughter, as well as momentary relief from pain and sorrow. Memories that were created years before, when reminisced in the light of joy and laughter, can ease the tension and heartache of sadness, increased stress, trauma, separation, or death. It is important to our happiness and therefore our *ever after*, to allow life's joys to pervade. There will never come a time that families will not need the healing balm of laughter.

My baby sister was born three months premature. My dad was on a business trip to Hawaii trying desperately to get home, and my mother was not doing well. It was a stressful, anxious, and terrifying situation for my parents and family. My dad made it to the hospital an hour after the baby was born, while all the children had been shipped off to other people's homes. Two days later, the stress was still at a peak level when my parents, sitting in the hospital, received a message that their daughter, Michelle, needed to be taken to the hospital. She had a severely broken arm from a roller skating accident and someone needed to pick her up or they would call an ambulance.

My mother relates that the hospital staff had gathered in her room. Things were tense at the hospital as my sister was not doing well. When my mother heard the news, she just started to laugh. It was either laugh or cry at this point as my mother had breached her emotional limit. Crying would have drained her already fatigued body and depressed her even more, but the laughter was soothing. The tension in the entire room released. In light of great uncertainty and fear, laughter brought hope and healing. It helped them to deal with the stress and still enjoy the crazy.

On a lighter note, laughter can strengthen family bonds by creating joyful memories. One Christmas as my family gathered together, my younger brother was reading a children's book. It was late, and I don't know what inspired my brother's ridiculous animation, but tears rolled down our faces as we shook with laughter at his drunken and slurred reading, when he in fact hadn't been drinking at all. He sounded like a broken record. He was laughing and crying so hard, he struggled to finish the story. Such a silly thing, but it brought us closer as we were simply able to enjoy a moment together. It somehow made us a bit more patient with each other.

When I was a child, my mother and I were watching a cartoon in which she clearly had become overly involved. As tension built and a character fumbled a magic potion, my mother cried out with deep emotion "Oh no! If he drops the vile he will never be turned back to normal!" My siblings and I laughed until our cheeks throbbed and our sides ached. You probably needed to be there to appreciate it. As my mom laughed along with us, I felt I understood her better, and because I could laugh with her, I felt I could trust her more. As I grew up, we had many more opportunities for unadulterated laughter, and not only did it draw us closer, but it helped us be more accepting of the silly and often maddening things we all did.

Laughing at our own mistakes and idiosyncrasies goes a long way toward maintaining a positive attitude and extending patience. We can lighten our loads by giving ourselves the benefit of the doubt. I often point out to my kids and spouse, and they point out to me, the mistakes I've made, and we really have a good laugh. We are not any less of a person because we make mistakes.

My husband's father learned this the hard way. As my husband remembers, "Everyone's eyes grew wide as the luggage scraped the ceiling and tumbled to the ground. The car came to a halt before it ever made it outside. We were five hours late leaving for our holiday vacation. Due to the freezing temperatures, Dad packed the luggage on top of the car while still inside the garage. In a rush and without thought to the height of the newly packed luggage, Dad pulled out of the garage. In a fury he got out to observe the damage. He could find nothing humorous in our current demise, but the sounds of laughter wafting from the car could not be ignored. Every time Dad opened the door the laughter was silenced only to begin again when the door closed. Eventually he was able to laugh and find peace and patience for himself and our family in the mess and damage he had created, and it is a wonderful memory."

If we can invite laughter into our homes, we will have happier families, because it will bring with it forgiveness, patience, trust, hope, and peace.

Serve

In family life, we don't want to feel like we are just another face in the crowd. We need to feel special, recognized, and loved. Oscar Wilde said it perfectly: "How can a woman be expected to be happy with a man who insists on treating her as if she were a perfectly normal human being?" (Wilde, 1908). I would add, how can a man be happy when his family treats him the same as the guy on the corner, or how can our kids feel special if we don't treat them like they are special? When we serve our family and give them the "royal treatment," it sets them apart from the maze of other people around us, and gives us more patience, love, and respect for them. Our children discover their self-esteem and the wonders of life through the people who love them and treat them like the princes and princesses they are.

We should constantly be aware of our family's needs and wishes and we should seek to fulfill them. This is our *ever after* and the people with us on the ride of our life and in our stories should be treated like royalty. After all, I've never seen a happily *ever after* where the royal family wasn't served and treated like royalty. Serving our families and doing nice things for them is a wonderful way to find joy in our *ever after* and increase our love and patience. Sometimes we may feel like the members in our family don't deserve acts of kindness. Sometimes they probably don't, but maybe if we treat them like they do, they soon will. People tend to better understand, appreciate, and love the people they serve, so who better to love and serve than your family?

I noticed one autumn that my daughter started layering her clothing. I thought it was a cute new style. I finally realized she was doing it because she had grown out of all of her sweatshirts and she was tired of being cold. The next time I went to the store I bought her a fleece sweater in her favorite color. It wasn't expensive, it didn't take me long, and she loved it. She was so grateful to me. I was so taken aback by her newfound bliss. Her happiness and gratitude inspired me to try a little harder to see what other things the members of my family needed.

If you know your husband has his sights set on a new iPad, save some money, or sell some junk. It is okay to give up something you want for someone else. When people take time and effort to sacrifice on your behalf, it is humbling and flattering. My brother and his wife shared their story:

"On the back of our bathroom door, we have three towel hooks. My husband and I each desire two for our individual towel, which allows it to dry faster and more completely, but this leaves the other of us with only one hook. We would battle over this and came up with the system [that] whoever hangs up their towel first gets two hooks. After a while, I noticed that my husband started to deliberately leave me two hooks for my towel, and taking only one for his own. I felt so special. This simple deed continued and I joined in. Now, whoever hangs up their towel first takes only one hook and honors the other with two. It is such a small act, but it means so much. Every time I hang my towel on the two hooks he left me, I think, 'He loves me.' Similarly, every time I choose to hang my towel on one hook and give him two, I think about how much I love him. It is a simple joy that brings me happiness every day."

This couple knew that neither he nor she was more important than the other, and neither were their needs. They both deserved two hooks. By deciding to give up his towel hook, just because, his wife felt special and loved and vice versa.

Money isn't always a luxury and so when I feel fiscally pinched I often look for alternative ways to serve my family. I have found that giving my time is often the more meaningful sacrifice. Skipping out on your favorite sitcom to help your child clean their room would be wonderful. Going on a walk with your wife instead of checking emails could make all the difference. In family relationships there are endless opportunities to do kind things and to show love.

Whenever I think of treating loved ones like royalty, I think of the Sheppard family. My Uncle Lee battled with a lifelong kidney disease. His father died from it, so Lee had a very real understanding of his fate. When his kidneys shut down, they were removed; he began dialysis and went onto a kidney donor list. Months later, Pam, his wife, went into surgery to donate her kidney to her husband. This was no small act of service. She spent a great deal of effort losing weight and getting her body into good enough condition to qualify herself as a kidney match. She knew there were great risks, but her husband was her king and she longed to give this gift to him. To her, he was royalty and there was no one more worthy of such a sacrifice. The surgery went astoundingly well for both her and her husband. No one made her do this, but her entire family, including herself, will be forever grateful.

This is an unusual example. It is quite unlikely that most of us will need to fill a need of this magnitude, but maybe treating our family like the royalty they are will help us become the kind of people courageous enough to make such a sacrifice.

Create Special Occasions

Often life seems to drag even when we are running at immeasurable speeds. When this happens I try to increase my patience and enjoy my family by creating special occasions. Maybe you need to get dressed up for a night out with your sweetheart or maybe you need to take your thirteen-year-old to the movies. For our special occasions we created Fun Fridays. It is a mini theme party we have every Friday. My kids love it and always look forward to it. My husband plays "monster night" with the kids, chasing them around in the darkness and jumping out at them for a fun scare. It could be as simple as fixing an Italian themed meal with a stunning table or having a finger food feast. Most of us put a lot of effort into our relationships with friends and it's time we did the same for our families. We need to make life special for the ones we love.

Make Your House a Marvelous Home

A home is a place we want to be—or at least a place we should want to be. The physical state of our home largely influences our happiness and patience. Where we live and how it makes us feel have everything to do with our *family ever after*. It should be our base, safe house, haven, and castle of sorts. It is a place where happiness should reside.

I have often observed how and where children play, and children don't enjoy messes. They love making messes, but they don't want to clean it up and they don't want to play in a room if it's already messy. My children will go for weeks without using their playroom if it is too messy, but as soon as it is cleaned up, organized, and in order, they want nothing else but to create imaginary and magical worlds in that same room.

This is how I feel about my house and the way it looks. Its appearance not only affects my ever-changing mood, but it plays a large role as to whether my life flows easily or is halted because I can't find the kids' homework, I stub my toe on a toy, or my shoe goes missing just as I'm running out the door. We clean our homes for visitors because we want them to feel safe and comfortable in our home, and we want them to be at ease and enjoy themselves. It only makes sense to create such an atmosphere for our families. We all need the security and peace a clean and organized home provides.

For a short time I became engrossed in a TV show that featured people who hoarded objects and pets in their homes. They didn't organize, throw things away, or clean things up. The decorations they did have were lost and destroyed in the heaps of junk they treasured. Their piles of purses, crafts, tools, collectibles, and clothes ate away at their happily *ever afters*, until their *ever afters* crumbled and their roller coaster carts derailed. Husbands left wives, children were removed from their homes, and the grandkids were not allowed over, all because their homes were in disarray. I understand this type of hoarding is a disorder and is not easily remedied, but the reason I bring it up is to show how much the physical state of our home affects family relationships, patience with our loved ones, and happiness.

Take the time to de-junk. I don't want to come home to a mess every day, or spend my time relocating useless items from corner to corner. We need to create spaces to live life in, not spaces we can't walk around in or spaces that hide the things we really need. Get organized so you know where things are, and decorate your house so it feels like a home.

Hang the pictures you love and display the knick-knacks you just can't part with. Create spaces you and your family find irresistible, not spaces you have to tolerate and trip over.

This doesn't take barrels of money, and your idea of home is going to be different than that of others. I am okay with a little clutter if it means I get to do puzzles with my kids, but I don't like to feel crowded. Using different colored paint on my walls feels warm to me, but to my dad, white paint is home, and feels clean and tidy. Use what you have. Remove what is too old, worn, or dirty, or fix it up a bit. It is amazing what a fresh coat of paint can do or maybe just a good dusting.

Be creative. I have what used to be beautiful wingback chairs in my living room. Over the years, my children's dirty rough feet have sullied them and they have become worn on the armrests. I covered the wear and tear with cute pillows, and now I can enjoy the room again. Even an old apartment can feel like a home if you give it, and the people in it, some tender loving care.

I don't want cleaning and organizing to be the culmination of my life. We need to keep our perspective and maintain balance in our effort to make our house a home. My home doesn't have to be spick and span for me to want to be there, but when I can keep things clean, be organized, and surround myself with the things I love, family life is so much more manageable and far less crazy.

I think we can all learn a lot from newlyweds. They are forever being intentional. They are positive and optimistic about their new life together. They laugh at everything and constantly find opportunities to serve each other. They leave notes on each other's cars, give each other gifts, and make time to go to lunch together. I remember coming home on our first Valentine's Day to our studio apartment filled with balloons and flowers. It made me feel so special. Newlyweds create special occasions by eating ice cream for breakfast or having spur of the moment food fights, just because it's fun. They sleep in just to cuddle and they take time to make their new house a home by adorning it with the things they love. Family life will always have twists and turns. There will be crazy times when we feel our frayed rubber bands will snap, but it can still be wonderful if we find ways to enjoy it.

CHAPTER TEN

Extending the Love

Challenge: Reach out to improve a relationship with an extended family member

Extended Family and In-Laws Can Be a Support in Times of Need

Talking about extended families—parents, siblings, in-laws, aunts, uncles, cousins, and for this book's purpose, any other family who is not, you, your spouse or your children—can be a Pandora's Box. Everyone seems to have a love/hate relationship with the in-laws who always give unwanted advice, or the brother who borrows money. Extended family can be difficult to deal with and many people avoid their in-laws, parents, even their siblings like the plague. There are likely many well-founded reasons for this, but it makes me sad. I love my extended family. They all have their quirks, but they are fabulous and so vitally important in my version of *family ever after*.

Loving From a Distance

Much of what we learn of good and bad stems from the homes we grew up in. We learn how to treat our family members by what we see our parents, grandparents, aunts, and uncles do. Maybe you are lucky like me and have an incredibly un-baggaged family, or maybe you are wondering, like many others, how can I love them from a distance?

Anna tells of the constant battle of loving her family, showing respect, and maintaining healthy boundaries. Anna grew up in what most would consider a dysfunctional home. She didn't enjoy her home life because there was great strife between her parents, who eventually divorced. The contention between her parents created an atmosphere prone to bouts of fighting and lasting resentment amongst all family members. When her parents separated, home life improved even though her mother still used manipulative and inappropriate parenting techniques. She learned to cope and find some happiness, but it wasn't until Anna took a class in college about family and parenting did she understand that her mother had crossed many parent-child boundaries, and that she and her mother did not have a normal or healthy relationship.

She spoke of the pain that her mother created by treating her more like a friend instead of a daughter, slipping in subtle and not so subtle attacks on her already fragile self-esteem, and even trying to take over her friendships by being such a cool "mom." The day Anna overheard her friend tell her mother that she (Anna's mother) "was so much cooler than Anna," broke her heart. There was enough for her to worry about in teenhood that she didn't want to have to compete with her mother for friends. Anna pleaded with her mother to stop making friends with her friends and boyfriends, but the desire for boundaries was ignored. Even now that Anna is an adult married with children, she tells of the constant miscommunications that continue to occur in their relationship and how she feels her mother is unwilling to take responsibility for her own life. She describes her discouragement about the relationship and the relationship games her mother plays that no one else knows the rules to.

Anna so badly wants a healthy, loving relationship with her mother but has realized that she must find happiness despite her actions and dysfunctions. She feels she can't control situations, but she can control her own actions and be willing to forgive herself and other people. Anna put it this way:

"I am responsible for behaving appropriately with the family my husband and I have created. I am responsible for loving my mother and showing kindness and respect, but I will not take responsibility for my mother's emotional state or her actions. I have given myself permission not to worry about whether or not she is judging me or thinks I'm a bad person because she doesn't agree with my personal beliefs or ways of doing things."

"Looking back on my childhood, I think what I really did was 'learn the eggshells': where it was okay to tread, where to tread lightly, and where to avoid. Growing up, certain topics of conversation would produce immediate defensiveness and contention. Changing how I look at life has been a lot of what I've done since I moved away from home. I now live with a family philosophy that there are no eggshells and that it is okay to talk about any topic as long as respect and sensitivity are maintained. I think it is really healthy to evaluate your paradigm and make changes; it's also extremely difficult. It is so hard to encounter eggshells when you've decided that they shouldn't exist."

A continual process for Anna is discovering the dysfunctions of her extended family inside of her. She admits that some of the dysfunctional traits are harder for her to let go of than others. It has been a constant battle of hope and internal torment as she struggles to forgive herself and family members for the misdeeds of her youth and move on, while continuing to forgive the ever-present disagreements, arguments, and injustices that present themselves. She knows that true happiness for her will come through forgiveness of herself and family members, and she knows this will be a constant progression.

Many of us come from homes and families like this. Even if our parents or siblings never change, we can. Like Anna, we can break the chains of dysfunction rooted inside us. Through our example and diligence, we can create for future generations an extended family that supports, even if it need be from a distance. Alexander Pope said, "A man should never be ashamed to own that he has been in the wrong, which is but saying in other words, that he is wiser today than he was yesterday" (Swift, 1739). We can look at our parents' lives, our grandparents' lives, and our own lives and change what does not bring our current families true happiness. If we do not learn from our past, we are doomed to repeat it.

If I have any one great hope for my children and their families, it is that they will be able to improve on the life they found with us. I hope that they will be able to weed out the dysfunction and find a happier, better way. We can become the kind of parents, grandparents, siblings, and family members who are able to give and receive support if it is offered.

Like Anna, we can learn to find peace and love in our extended families whether or not they are willing to change. Boundaries must often be set, but I truly believe our extended families, for the most part, can improve our *ever after*.

A Network of Love

We need to be willing to take initiative in building relationships with extended family, and possibly in mending wounded relationships. We might have to be the ones who start the rippling effect of love. When my husband and I were married, my in-laws intimidated me. This was no fault of their own—I just didn't know them well. Our lack of familiarity caused me to keep an emotional and physical distance. They accepted me just the way I was and put forth their best effort to build a relationship with me, but I was timid with their attempts.

I am ashamed to admit that at times, I looked for their faults and blamed them for many of my husband's idiosyncrasies. I know that I hurt their feelings, though unintentionally, but they loved me anyway. It was not until I decided to make an effort to show love, appreciation, patience, and kindness that our relationship could progress.

When it comes to the in-laws and extended family, keep in mind that marrying into a family is really like being adopted. Bonds don't just form they must be created. We have to be willing to build a relationship. We need to realize that our new family has different ways of doing things. They may like different foods, they may watch movies instead of play games, or they may be Republicans rather than Democrats. The options are endless, but these differences do not have to inhibit our ability to love this new family.

We need to make an effort to show respect to them, just as we would want them to do for us. They are not always the reason our husband or wife do annoying things, but even if they are, let it go. We need to look outside our world and realize we also are a product of our parents and the family we grew up in.

Don't waste your time blaming extended family for problems. If they do something you really don't like, change that in your own family. You can still love them and maintain boundaries. You can still love them and be your own family. You can still love them and be the parent you want to be. Working with and learning to appreciate and love extended family is not going to be love at first sight. It takes massive amounts of patience, willingness, forgiveness, and acceptance. It is a lifelong endeavor.

In the midst of raising a family and trying to have a good relationship with my spouse, my husband and I have relied heavily on the teachings and wisdom of our extended family. We have healthy relationships with them, and their experiences are a treasure to us. They have been where we have been and they have learned a great deal from their successes and failures in their own families. They don't expect us to take all their counsel or do everything they say. They let us make our own mistakes, and, just as my parents did when I was young, they help us when we've been caught in a trap.

I often see a tendency to put down the wisdom of our parents and grandparents, using the excuse that they don't know what they are talking about. Though this may be true when it comes to technology, their life experience has given them wisdom, not made them out of touch. The fact that they have made mistakes just makes them more likely to realize in retrospect what the wiser choice would have been. Of course they are still imperfect people, but so are we. Maybe if we combine what we know with what they know, we will all be better people, with better homes and better families.

My husband and I have asked our parents' opinions on numerous parenting techniques and financial decisions, such as buying a home. We have appreciated their counsel but know the decisions we make as well as their consequences are ours. We need to keep in mind, we are our own families and seeking advice from others is important, but they should not be making the decisions for us, or come between us. When our spouse feels we should take one path and our parents feel differently, it is wise to side with our spouse not Mom or Dad. Our spouse is our first priority, not our parents. My sister-in-law put it this way:

"Your spouse is who you will live with the rest of your life. If your plan is to get divorced and move back in with your parents, then listen to them even when it's at odds with your spouse. If your goal is to stay married, listen to, and side with, your spouse over your parents. Give your spouse priority and your deepest consideration, over anyone else."

When you are the in-law, parent, or grandparent, keep in mind your boundaries. It is not my parents' job to raise my children or maintain a good relationship with my spouse. It is my job. I have seen couples separated because, in time of marriage crisis, the parents pulled the couple away from each other rather than teaching them love and patience. I am definitely not suggesting parents' support abusive behavior in families, but separating the family is likely the most destructive thing you can do, especially for children. Try to teach them a better way.

One woman, who was a wonderful friend, began to question the integrity of her marriage. She was feeling depressed and unsure of her feelings towards her husband. Her parents wanted to protect her, and in their desire to defend her, they continually pushed for a separation. Her parents struggled to find any redeemable qualities in their son-in-law, and ultimately saw the solution to their problems was found in dissolving the marriage. As the pressure to get divorced increased, the couple terminated the marriage, as well as any chance of a happily *ever after* with each other. I watched from the sidelines as this divorce wreaked havoc on their tender hearts, for both husband and wife. They seemed to question their motives and constantly wondered if they could have made the marriage work.

Interestingly enough, we had another good friend presented with a very similar circumstance, but as their parents took a more positive approach, the marriage was able to triumph. When this woman went to her parents for counsel, heartbroken at her husband's treatment of her, their first questions were, "Do you still love him?" "Are you physically safe?" "Are you willing to do whatever it takes to make this work?" When all questions were answered in the affirmative, her parents feeling her pain and very much concerned for his happiness took a different approach than our other friend. They resisted the urge to criticize her husband and instead helped her to look for the positive in him. They told her to go to her husband and try to work things out. They had both love and compassion for daughter and son-in-law, and their wise counsel helped them save their marriage. I do not know exactly what our friends did to work out their misgivings and allow happiness to return to their marriage, but I do know the counsel of their parents impacted them greatly.

As extended family members, and especially parents, we have great desires to protect our loved ones. We need to examine if the enactment of our desires to protect our loved ones is really helping. We should encourage our families when things are really hard, and avoid voicing critical and thoughtless remarks. When our friend's parents took a more positive approach with their son and son-in-law, it resulted in a happier outcome. Marriages do not usually come with a built-in villain and a preceding victim. They are usually made of two amazing and imperfect people who don't know how to forgive and get along. We should be the kind of extended family who help their families' relationships rather than hurt them.

We should tread softly when it comes to our children's, siblings', and other extended family relationships. Be wise. There are extreme circumstances such as abuse or adultery in which a parent or extended family member would need to intervene, where counseling would be necessary, and possibly the consideration of divorce appropriate. But we shouldn't be the parent or family member who is the tipping point of destruction when there are other healthier, happier solutions. When in doubt, air on the side of love and hope, and consult a professional if needed.

When it comes to your extended family—parents, children, siblings, grandparents etc.—remember the profound influence you have in your family's lives. Be positive and wise, don't meddle where you have no business, and be a support when needed.

Safe Support

Often extended family can be just what the doctor ordered. My brother-in-law struggled in his teenage years. After discussing with his parents, he decided to move in with my husband and me. We loved the time we had with him. We enjoyed getting to know him better and he enjoyed the change of pace and freedom he felt living away from home. It gave him the opportunity to reevaluate his life without the pressures of parents and old friends. He is now a great man doing great things with his life. Sometimes extended family can break barriers and boundaries parents cannot. Be the kind of family member your extended family can rely on when times are tough.

After buying our first house, it flooded severely. We didn't have anywhere to go. Our grandparents let us live in their basement for three months while we cleaned up the mess and remodeled. They would babysit our two children while we worked late into the night. They made us delicious food when we had little time, money, or energy to prepare our own. They listened when we were discouraged and were patient when we were annoying. They were a saving grace for us.

When we started a new company and had no money, siblings dropped fresh fruit at the door, mailed gift cards, or sent cash. They would come visit us so we wouldn't have to spend the extra gas to go visit them. My grandparents cleaned out their pantry into ours and Bryce's grandparents dropped an envelope of money into our hands. Aunts and uncles sent money for Christmas, or offered to pay gas money so we could afford to attend our grandparents' fiftieth wedding anniversary, and our parents even paid a few of our bills, all with no strings attached. They helped us when we were in our hardest moments. Their concern for us was motivated by love, not duty. We should let the motivations for our actions with our extended family be that of love with no strings attached.

When I became seriously ill due to a heart condition, my sister and brother-in-law came to watch my kids whenever they could, and my brother and his wife, kept our fridge stocked with heart-healthy meals. As I was resting a few days after my trip to the Emergency Room, I looked out the window to find my pregnant sister-in-law, Liz, with her three boys parked in my driveway. She and her husband felt they wanted to help in some way, so she got in the car and drove two days across the country to come and take care of me. My husband and I were overwhelmed by the sacrifices our extended family made in our behalf.

On a recent outing with my husband's family, we braved the Vedauwoo rocks in Wyoming. There were eleven kids under age twelve, and we all climbed the mountain to the top. It was amazing to me how aunts and uncles stepped in to help, how brothers worked together to pull and push people up the rocks, and how mothers, sisters, and grandparents held little hands that were not always their own children. We were able to hand kids down from person to person in order to get the children safely up or down steeper slopes. Everyone looked out for everyone, and we made it up and down without a single injury. I knew if my child was with any of the other family members they would be safe.

I couldn't help but compare this to life. This is what extended family is for—they should be a support. They should continually look out for each other and help one another not just because they are asked or because it's convenient. I can assure you it was not convenient for pregnant Liz to drive across the country to help me or for my other siblings and their spouses to show up at my house with food and take care of my children for days on end. It was not convenient for parents, siblings, grandparents, aunts, and uncles to share their hard-earned food, money, and time. Just as we were all concerned for the well-being and safety of everyone on that mountain, we, as extended family, should constantly be aware of our loved ones and their well-being and safety. Had we only looked out for our own families while on the mountain, I am quite positive we would have had a far greater struggle, and likely not made it to the top. Nor would it have ended without injury.

Life, like climbing a mountain, is definitely rocky at times. It is hard work and often very tiring. We can't do it alone. Having loved ones at our side helps us achieve beyond our own capabilities. It helps us discover that we can do things we didn't believe we could, and it helps us find joy even when it is hard. I am grateful that I am part of such great families and hope that I can be a support to them just as they are to me.

Extended family relations can be festering with open wounds. We can't make our relationships or our relatives change, but we can have an influence for good. Coldness, unconcern, and uncaring actions won't change anything. We need to love them and find ways to help them. They have trials just as we do. Think how much it means, or would mean, if someone helped our struggling teenager through a tough time, babysat our children so we could have a date, remembered our birthday, helped us move, or just listened when we were having a bad day. We have families for a reason. They can provide us with unimaginable support, and we in turn have the opportunity to make a difference for the people we love, and we should do it.

CHAPTER ELEVEN

Love Fosters Love

*Challenge: Show love to your spouse or child
the way they feel loved*

Love Them Their Way

I spend hours taking care of the kids, beautifying the home, scrubbing bathrooms, making dinners, chauffeuring children, helping with homework, and supplementing our income. After such a long day of slaving away and trying to please everyone, I feel like my husband should automatically know how much I love him. After all, I did all those things for him, right? So I must ask myself why he isn't groveling at my feet in love and gratitude.

As I pondered this question, I realized I don't actually do all of those things for him. When I look a little deeper into my motives, I realize that all of those responsibilities are a natural consequence of the life I chose—they are requirements. I take care of my kids because I'm a mom and I do my job because it's my job. Why don't I grovel at his feet for being a successful businessman? I do appreciate what he does and I know he works hard, just as I know he appreciates me, and the work I do. These are important jobs that if not performed would cause hardships, but these are not the actions that keep a relationship thriving. I don't feel loved by my husband because he makes cool apps or puts in some great kitchen lighting for someone else. He doesn't feel loved when I do the dishes or take the kids to school. He feels loved when I hold him, when he feels my touch. I feel loved when he takes me on dates and helps around the house and tells me he loves me.

I can assure you that if the only traits my husband used to dazzle me while courting me were his great work ethic and good looks I would have walked the other way. It's not that those weren't great traits but I wouldn't have felt like he really loved me. My craftiness, curves, and motivation would not have sealed the deal for him if I didn't find plenty of opportunities to hug and kiss him. He would have been left wondering, "Does she really love me?" It is important to do the drudgework of life, but it is more important to take the time to love your loved ones in a way that makes them feel loved.

One of our friends was headed out of town for a few days. In an effort to show his love (or maybe to kiss up), he scheduled and paid for a massage for his wife. This gesture of love was very real and very thoughtful. Him leaving on his business trip to help support their family did not make her feel loved, but her husband's gift did. Similarly, my dad often travels and though the income that these trips provide benefits his wife, my mom does not feel loved by his frequent absences or his Herculean attempts to make money. She does, however, feel loved when he takes the time to call her and connect with her every night and every morning while he is away, because she knows it means he is thinking about her. These men had to go above and beyond their usual daily activities to show their love.

In an attempt to teach a group of girls about service and love, I threw an ice cream party. I set out a few different ice cream flavors, with all the toppings imaginable. I gave them each a dish and told them to make the best ice cream sundae conceivable. They were given strict instructions not to eat it. They had oodles of fun. When they were all done, I told them to give their ice cream sundae to the person sitting to their right. The room went silent. I heard comments like, "I don't like that flavor," "I hate nuts," and "this doesn't look very yummy." Then the teaching began.

The first thing I told them was that when they are trying to do loving and kind things for someone else, they need to think about what they are doing, and who they are doing it for. Consider their needs, their likes, and their loves. What if they are lactose intolerant? Just because you like caramel topping doesn't mean they will, but they may love strawberry.

The second lesson I taught them was that when someone does something kind in a gesture of love for them they need to accept the love. It may not be exactly what you would have picked, but they put effort into their gift and they did it because they care. Don't deny the gift because you don't like vanilla flavored ice cream or coconut. It is always best to show gratitude.

The third lesson was to be sure they found joy in their service. They could have just as much fun making ice cream sundaes for the girl next to them as they did when they made it for themselves.

Early on in our marriage, I had my heart set on a leather purse from the mall. I decided it was out of my price range and did not make the purchase. As we went to the car, my husband pulled out the purse he had so stealthily purchased. He was tickled about his gift and was feeling pretty awesome for thinking of me. As his brother watched from the sidelines, I denied the gift. I was upset at him for buying something we couldn't afford and told him to take it back. Entirely embarrassed and hurt, he handed me the purse and got in the car. He was thoughtful about the purchase he made, thinking only of how much I would love it. I, however, "spilled" the love, as my dad would say, with my unwillingness to accept his gift. I felt about as little as a mouse and quickly learned to accept the love and gestures my family offered. I loved that purse and used it for ten years before I tucked it away in my closet. Every time I used it I was reminded of the love my husband had for me.

Next time your wife makes a nice meal just for you and she burns it, don't be rude or ungrateful—accept the gift. The next time your husband does the dishes and leaves the counters filled with crumbs and the pots and pans next to the sink, say thank you, instead of nitpicking the imperfections. Next time your kids plant a seed for you that never grows, express your gratitude.

When I was a little girl, I was bubbling with excitement to give my dad his Christmas present. I had gotten a shoebox and carefully cut out hearts to go inside. When my Dad opened the shoebox my heart sank—there were no hearts, just an empty box. My dad was careful not to "spill the love" and showed immediate gratitude for the empty box. There were no sarcastic remarks made or a chuckle at my innocent naivety. He gave me a hug and told me he loved it. I never did figure out what happened to my hearts, but I have always remembered how careful my dad was with my heart, and how accepting he was of the love I had tried to give him.

Everyone feels loved in different ways. Our kids don't always feel loved because we make them breakfast or drive them to school, even if the only reason we do it is because we love them. My kids feel loved when I paint their nails or read them stories, when I play ball with them or show up at their recitals and games. They feel loved when I let them have their friends over or cry with them when they get bullied at school. They feel loved when I spend time just with them. We need to pay attention to how our loved ones feel loved and make the extra effort to love them their way.

What is Love?

My daughter told me once that her friend wished I were her mom. This intrigued me as I know her mother and I know she loves her children very much and is a wonderful mother. I asked my daughter why this was. The answer was straightforward; "you buy us toys." Suddenly I felt very inadequate in my parenting. My daughter didn't realize that the accumulation of stuff or activities doesn't constitute love. We want to buy things for our children because we love them, but if we don't have extra money to buy things for our kids, it doesn't mean they aren't well cared for or very loved. Most people already know that having things doesn't equate love but sometimes we need a reminder.

We could spend all the money in the world on stuff and never have anyone's love in return. Love is shown through paying attention to our family and investing time for the

172   Family Ever After

things that matter most. It is found in the words we speak and the actions we take in serving our family. It is found in our willingness to forgive and trust. It is found in patience. It is not always practical or convenient. Love is the purest form of charity and unselfishness. It is putting the welfare of another above ourselves. Love is treating and serving our family like the royalty they are.

Withered Without Love

Every time I gaze through my front windows, I feel a tinge of guilt as I see the dust and sticks that remain in my hanging flower baskets. This is a deep guilt that extends through many years of failed flower baskets. I love flowers—really, really love flowers—but it has become apparent that I do not love my flowers enough. The interesting thing about my flowers is that when I planted them they were good; the soil was good and the climate was right. They had everything they needed to be healthy, happy, and beautiful. I saved up my money to buy my flowers and I enjoyed planning how they would look in their lovely pots. I was very diligent in my upkeep, being sure to water them, fertilize them, and give them little breaks needed from the heat of the western desert sun. Over time I would miss a day here and a day there, knowing they would be fine. As the summer got busier, I began to fully neglect my flowers. They would wither and I would water them in hopes of revival. For the first month or so, the water would rejuvenate their withered frames, but each time I neglected them, they came back weaker than the time before. As the summer winds and storms came, my once beautiful flowers could not combat and eventually they were lost to the elements.

I soon realized how our families are so similar to my beloved flowers. When my family began, I was so excited. I planned the details of our life and was tender, intuitive, and careful with our new creation. Our family was good. I don't know many families or children who are not good in the beginning, just as the soil was good and the climate right with my flowers. We had everything we needed to grow and become breathtakingly beautiful. If we found something was amiss, we immediately sought out the needed bug spray or fertilizer to do the trick. Sometimes it was a date night, sometimes it was an apology, and sometimes it was a little service.

In the beginning, it was easy and enjoyable to nourish our growing family. We had the money, the time, and the motivation. Over time it became more difficult to show our effort, enthusiasm, and love. The more we neglected family life and tried to revive it, the weaker it became. As our blue skies darkened and a storm breached our marriage, we were on the verge of what some would consider a marital "deal breaker." When the storm passed, we were feeling withered from the intensity of the storm. We decided individually that we had invested in something incredible and we were not going to let our neglect and inability to love and forgive destroy it. So unlike my dead flowers we began to be consistent with our love. We intended to make a soil so powerful, so clean, and so strong, that no storm could penetrate it. We worked constant nourishment into our marriage. We rejuvenated our soil and created a strong home for our growing family, so the next time a storm came (and you can be sure it did) we would be prepared and continue to be lush and full of love.

The better our soil became, the deeper our roots of love secured themselves and grew together. Families are incredibly powerful and resilient when bonded in love, and can become durable and impenetrable. They are a support system that cannot be replaced. They can bring peace, joy, and happiness in a way that is incomparable to anything else. Focus on creating a root system in your marriage and family that will protect you from your own neglect and the circumstances that are out of your control that will come. No matter how strong our roots are, if we do not daily add to the soil of our homes and families, they will become prey to outside elements.

In America's days of slavery, slaveholders often cunningly separated families. Children were sold away from parents, as well as husbands away from wives. I think this was done because the slaveholders knew that strong family bonds created with love would lead to strength for the slaves, and if this happened it would make it incredibly difficult to maintain slavery. Individuals can easily be swayed and controlled, especially when they are overburdened with sorrow and hardship. But strong families bonded in love would rebel against their masters and the destruction they caused. There is power and happiness in families that show forth love. When we feel loved, we find strength in all aspects of our lives—when the western sun comes, we can enjoy its rays, rather than wither.

Help strengthen your family by teaching them love through your example. Love can pull your family through the greatest of life's hardships. If you want to show love to someone, serve them. Great bonds are built through service. It's hard not to love someone you are serving, and it's hard not to feel loved when you are the recipient of selfless service. If you want to destroy love, the surest and fastest route is selfishness. It is an unwillingness to share your material goods, time, love, friendship, and self. The media seems to bombard us at every turn, telling us that we should be looking out only for ourselves and that we will gain happiness by doing so. This is a lie. The only guarantee selfishness brings is a loss of what you love most.

I recently watched a commercial where a father and mother were out late playing and enjoying themselves. They were in their very expensive cars with their sexy clothing and having drinks with their fabulous friends. All this was played out while their son was at home searching for them. He was bored and a bit lonely. I'm not saying a night out on the town is bad; in fact, I love my nights out with the hubby. My point is simply this: the happiest families I see are the ones who continue to nourish and focus on family, not the ones who indulge themselves in fads, fun, and wealth. The intent of the commercial was to portray that you could have a perfect life by buying their perfect product. To me, however, it was a portrayal of misplaced priorities and selfishness. The commercial made me sad. There was no *family ever after* going on in that family. Long lasting and extraordinary happiness in family life does not come by accumulating stuff, having nice things, or being selfish with your life.

The interesting thing about the media is that it is usually based on misconceptions. It is acting. Whenever I watch a movie or TV show with my kids, and I sense tension and fear in them, my first instinct is to remind them that what they are seeing is not real. I tell them it is just a story, acted out or drawn with a pencil. The happiness the media portrays for families is usually not real happiness. I am not really happy when my family is sad or lonely. I am not really happy to have a huge house or expensive cars if it means my husband and I never get to see each other because we have to work so much to pay for our expensive life. My husband is not really happy when I treat his remarks with sarcasm, and my kids are not really happy when I ignore them. We have got to keep in touch with reality, with what is real in our world, with what has the ability to bring the most happiness to our lives, and that is most definitely our families.

The Choice to Be Happy

It is a truth that our choices affect our happiness. It is truth that certain things will make us happier than others. Every choice we make has a consequence. We cannot choose what happens when we ignore our children or spouse because we are busy, tired, or consumed with other things.

My aunt Sandy brought up the point: "It is hard to be married. It is hard to have children. It is hard to be divorced. It is hard to be single." Life is hard no matter what path we choose, but we can always choose to be happy. We can choose to work on a having a happily *ever after* or we can choose to let it go because it is too hard. If we choose to let our *ever after* go, it's still going to be hard. Choose the path in life that will bring the most happiness not just to you but also to your family. Choose to put effort into being happy despite the hardships, twists, and turns on your roller coaster. Whether or not you find and live happily *ever after* is up to you.

As families, we are drawn to each other. We come from the same soil; it runs through our roots. No matter what life brings, who we are has everything to do with the families we come from. Their effects on us are lasting, and even if we are transplanted into another pot or get in a new roller coaster cart, our bonds cannot be broken. Take the time to make positive, healthy bonds. Bonds you can enjoy and bonds you want to remember.

The Rippling Effect of Love

When love is shown, it is natural to reciprocate. My children often make loving gestures to my husband or me when they see us showing love to them and each another. I can't think of a better place to learn about love than from your parents. As parents, we are the examples. There were numerous times as I was growing up that my siblings and I were grossed out while our parents kissed in the kitchen. Now, my children often make the same faces we did. I know my parents love each other and I'm quite sure my children know I love my husband.

One evening my son woke up confused about the time. Thinking that it was morning he said with a smile on his face, "Good morning, my love." It made me smile because it is what I say to the kids every morning upon waking. Our families recognize love in the home and often it gives them a desire to return such love. When I was pregnant with my third child and not feeling well, I lay down to rest. Lunch was still out and the kitchen was messy. When I woke up, lunch was put away and the counters cleared. I felt so loved by my daughter. She told me she knew I was tired and that she thought this might help. I loved feeling so loved, and I automatically wanted to show my love to her.

When I was a teenager my friend asked me if there was anyone I liked or thought was cute. I thought about it and named one person. Sensing something was afoot, I pressed for more information. I finally got it out of her that someone was interested. Knowing that this boy liked me made me like him. Funny, but I think this response is a very natural and real part of human nature. When someone loves you, it is hard not to love him or her back. It is like throwing a pebble in a pond and watching it spread.

A good friend related a life lesson to me about her experience at a water park:

"They have a new slide that accommodates eight separate riders at once and requires foam mats to ride on. Riders are told to lay stomach down on the mats and hold on tight. Children are allowed on the ride, but instead of lying down on the mat with your child, you have to sit up, put the child between your legs, and hold on to them. The first time we went down the ride, the operator firmly declared, 'Hold on to your kid, not the mat.' As we pushed off and butterflies filled my stomach my first instinct was to grab the slide to slow us down or to grab on to the mat to keep us stable on it. In a split second I made the decision to listen to the counsel I was given and wrap my arms around my little girl. It was exhilarating and scary. As we rode down I realized that whatever happened, we were in it together—even if that meant flying off the mat and completely wiping out—we would do it together. Subsequent ride operators informed us that there were times when a parent chose to hang on to the mat instead of their child and the child went flying off and was injured. 'It's happened,' he said. In that same split second I chose to wrap my arms around my child I realized that's what life is all about—we cling to our family and are in it together no matter what. We may slip up and even wipe out, but what matters is that we forgive each other and stay closely bonded, never giving up that bond for anything."

Life is a fast paced-ride. When we cling to our possessions, work, hobbies, addictions, possessions, and even friends, our happiness in our family and, in turn, life can slip away. Hold your family tighter when you think family life is getting away from you. Listen better and love more. Don't let go when things get scary; hang on because it's worth the ride.

As newlyweds, my husband and I were racing through Wyoming on our way to visit family. He was driving like a crazy man. This was serious business to him. He couldn't enjoy the eight-hour drive, because he was so worried about the cars around him. He passed every car he could and envisioned blowing up the rest of them so they would get out of his way. If a semi-truck pulled out in front of him, he would growl with dissatisfaction. I started laughing at him, and said, "Hon, this isn't a race. It's okay if another car passes us, or if a semi slows us down. It's going to happen. What is important is that we get to our destination safely, and enjoy the ride.

Life isn't a race against every other family—it is a journey. Let's not spend the ride of our life speeding through in a daze, unable to enjoy the people who are most important to us. Can we do better than we were doing? Can we be more efficient? Can we show our families how much we love them? What matters is that we are improving, that we are making an effort. Don't waste your time comparing your family with the billions of others on earth. You will always find yourself wanting. I often tell my children when they get in their competitive mode that there will always be someone ahead of them and someone in the rear. What is important is that they do their best. My mother always reminds me, "You can't know what is going on in someone else's home and life and it is not fair to them or you to compare."

Recently, as I brought a cup of water to my mouth, my daughter jumped on my lap and hit the cup. The glass flew through the air, spilling everywhere. My sister was visiting and could see I was about to lose my cool. She wisely said, "Red Punch, Red Punch, Red Punch!" I started to laugh. She had me. It was the perfect reminder. It was just a little spilled water. Having a happy family is an ongoing process. More drinks will be spilled, more feelings hurt, more stress that must be laughed away, more forgiveness that must be shown, more family memories to make, and more love to show. Making your *family ever after* happy is worth it. It's worth the effort and it's worth the time. My parents always used to tell me: "Friends come and go, but family is forever." Choose to live your happily *ever after* with your family. As the plaque on my piano so perfectly states, "It's never too late to live *Happily Ever After*."

Bibliography

The Arbinger Institute. *The Anatomy of Peace: Resolving The Heart of Conflict* (San Francisco, CA: Berrett-Koehler Publishers, Inc., 2006).

The Arbinger Institute. *Leadership and Self-Deception* (San Francisco, CA: Berrett-Koehler Publisher, Inc., 2010).

Dixon, Dr. Decia. "Kindness the Road to Personal and Family Fulfillment?" Happy Children and Families, last modified August 21, 2012, http://happychildrenandfamilies. com/2012/08/21/kindness-the-road-to-personal-and-family-fulfillment/.

Egan, Kerry. "My Faith: What People Talk about before They Die." CNN, last modified January 28, 2012, http://religion.blogs.cnn.com/2012/01/28/my-faith-what-people-talk-about-before-they-die/.

Harris, Sydney J. "Sydney J. Harris Quotes." Brainy Quotes, last modified 2013, http://www.brainyquote.com/quotes/authors/s/sydney_j_harris.html.

Hubbard, Elbert. "Goal Setting: Free Tutorial and Top Resources." About-Goal-Setting, last modified 2013, http://www.about-goal-setting.com.

Merton, Robert K. *Social Theory and Social Structure* (New York: Free Press, 1968).

Sherrin, Ned. *The Oxford Dictionary of Humorous Quotation* (New York: Oxford University Press Inc., 2008).

Swift, Johnathan. *Thoughts on Various Subjects* (London: Motte, Benjamin, 1727).

Wilde, Oscar. *A Woman of No Importance* (London: Methuen and Co., 1908).

William J. Doherty, Ph.D. *The Intentional Family: How to Build Family Ties in Our Modern World* (New York: Harper Collins, 1999).

About the Author

Michelle Packard is a mother to her four very human and totally fabulous kids: her oldest, Ella is always in charge and leads the pack with creativity and curiosity; Daniel follows with loyalty and loves tenderly; Julia is a doll and always buzzing over something beautiful; and Jackson could hunt down the last sharpie on earth to create art on your bathroom wall. Michelle has been married ten years and is quite taken with her guy. Date night is her favorite and she dreams of weekend getaways with her man. She loves creating beauty through floral design, but apparently has no gift with living flowers (they end of upside down and pressed in books). She finds parties alluring—they beckon her to invite people over, spend way too much time preparing food for murder mystery dinners, and totally enjoy friends and family. Michelle holds a bachelors degree in Home and Family Science from Brigham Young University. She has spent a great deal of time working with children and young adults and finds her greatest joy is happy families.

About Familius

Welcome to a place where mothers are celebrated, not compared. Where heart is at the center of our families, and family at the center of our homes. Where boo boos are still kissed, cake beaters are still licked, and mistakes are still okay. Welcome to a place where books—and family—are beautiful. Familius: a book publisher dedicated to helping families be happy.

Familius was founded in 2012 with the intent to align the founders' love of publishing and family with the digital publishing renaissance which occurred simultaneous with the Great Recession. The founders believe that the traditional family is the basic unit of society, and that a society is only as strong as the families that create it.

Familius' mission is to help families be happy. We invite you to participate with us in strengthening your family by being part of the Familius family. Go to www.familius.com to subscribe and receive information about our books, articles, and videos.

Website: www.familius.com
Facebook: www.facebook.com/paterfamilius
Twitter: @familiustalk, @paterfamilius1
Pinterest: www.pinterest.com/familius

CPSIA information can be obtained
at www.ICGtesting.com
Printed in the USA
FSOW01n1707190215
5259FS